# THE ILLUSTRATED

# POLICE NEWS

*For Cristina in Cebu –'mahal kita'*

## INTRODUCTION

*The Illustrated Police News (IPN) was, without a doubt, the most sensational newspaper of the mid and late-Victorian era. With a front cover often containing fine wood engravings of sea monsters, ghosts and sex-starved gorillas, it was guaranteed to appeal to a wide range of readers and non-readers alike.*

*Its main interest was of course crime, and murder in particular. With lurid illustrations of drunken axe-wielding assassins and their pathetic blood-soaked victims, the paper seemed to be daring the public to read the gory accounts inside.*

*Before the days of newspaper photographs the only likeness anybody saw of the infamous Victorian murderers was in papers like the IPN and their artists certainly had fertile imaginations. They would often depict the dreams of killers such as Kate Webster and showed details of the murder even though they rarely visited the scenes of the crimes*

*There was no doubt as to the biggest story the newspaper ever ran. We are all familiar with the events in Whitechapel in 1888 and the IPN devoted tens of thousands of words and many, many illustrations to the hunt for the Whitechapel murderer, now known as Jack the Ripper. Both illustrations and reports have featured heavily in films and books on the subject ever since.*

*These reprinted stories from the IPN are not just about crime, they cover the Victorians' fascination with animals, wacky pastimes and attitudes to foreigners and women. If you are interested in Victorian life, and lowlife in particular, there is no better reference work. Many of theses stories and illustrations are now reprinted for the first time, so if you can't get down to Colindale Newspaper Library to view the whole collection, please join us for a fascinating taster. All human and sub-human life was there.*

**Steve Jones, October 2002**

First published in October, 2002 by
**Wicked Publications**
222, Highbury Road,
Bulwell,
Nottingham
NG6 9FE
Telephone/Fax (0115) 9756828
e-mail: wickedbooks@ukonline.co.uk

ISBN 1-870000-08-0

*By the same author:*

**LONDON...THE SINISTER SIDE**

**WICKED LONDON**

**THROUGH THE KEYHOLE**

**CAPITAL PUNISHMENTS**

**IN DARKEST LONDON**

**WHEN THE LIGHTS WENT DOWN**

**NOTTINGHAM...THE SINISTER SIDE**

**MANCHESTER...THE SINISTER SIDE**

**BIRMINGHAM...THE SINISTER SIDE**

**NORTHUMBERLAND AND DURHAM...
THE SINISTER SIDE**

**LANCASHIRE LASSES...
THEIR LIVES AND CRIMES**

*see back pages for details*

*Typeset and printed in Great Britain by:*
*PARKER AND COLLINSON LIMITED*
*incorporating DESA DESIGN & PRINT*
*Church Street  Lenton  Nottingham  NG7 2FH*

# CONTENTS

## COMPILER'S NOTES

The first copy of the *IPN* appeared in 1864 and we have included stories from every decade of the nineteenth century. Unfortunately the illustrations of the 1890's are far inferior to the earlier ones so this decade is not so fully represented.

Although not complete, the most comprehensive collection of back copies of the *IPN* is at the National Newspaper Library in Colindale, North London.

When I first started researching in 1985 you could read the actual newspapers. Recently, because of their deteriorating condition, they have been transferred to film and are available for readers in that form at the library. The illustrations in this book have all been reproduced from film kept at Colindale. Unfortunately some of the better illustrations have been laminated and are therefore unsuitable for reproduction.

The headlines, text, grammar and spellings are as our ancestors would have read more than one hundred years ago. I have split the reports into paragraphs to make their reading easier on the eye.

Where possible I have researched the stories in other newspapers to find out the results of the court cases. Any italics are my contribution and did not appear in the *IPN*.

**STEVE JONES**, Nottingham, October, 2002

## ASSAULT BY SHOEBLACK

Patrick McQuin, a boy who has been for some time a shoeblack with a box and brushes in Leman-street, Whitechapel, was brought before Mr. Paget, charged with violently assaulting Mr. Abraham Woolf, a gentleman of the Jewish persuasion. The prosecutor is a traveller and jewel manufacturer, of 13, Everard-place, Back Church-lane, Whitechapel.

For some time past on leaving home in the mornings he has been pestered by the prisoner and other boys with boxes, brushes, and blacking to clean his boots. He had told them repeatedly that he did not want his boots cleaned, as they had been done at home. He was generally received with derision and laughter, his foreign dialect was mimicked, and the boys at last resorted to threats and abuse.

On Tuesday morning the prosecutor was assailed by the prisoner with the usual old cry of, "Clean your boots, sir, clean your boots, only a penny." Mr. Woolf told him he did not want his boots cleaned, on which the prisoner struck him down. Mr. Woolf was immediately surrounded by other shoebox boys to the number of six or seven. They hustled him and the prisoner kicked him on the mouth and cut it. The complainant immediately seized the prisoner and took him to the station-house.

Mr. Woolf's mouth was cut, and blood was issuing from it while giving his evidence.

Mr. Paget: When did this take place?

The prosecutor: At ten o'clock this morning – only an hour and a half ago.

The prisoner, whose face was scratched and bruised, said that Mr. Woolf beat him up, and clawed his neck and face.

Police-sergeant Fry, 658 A, said that the scratches were old ones and were quite dry. They had been made some time ago. Mr. Paget looked at the prisoner's face and neck and said Fry was quite correct. He commented on the conduct of the prisoner, and said he had no right to annoy or molest people who would not have their boots cleaned, but he would allow him and other boys to civilly accost people who wanted their boots cleaned. A flagrant and cowardly assault had been committed, and he sentenced the prisoner to one month's imprisonment and hard labour.

(02.03.1867)

# A CAT DEFENDING ITS MISTRESS

A very remarkable case came before Mr. Knox, at the Marlborough Police-court, some few days since. The facts sworn to are in themselves melancholy and revolting enough, albeit we must admit that the assault cases which come before the several Police-courts in the metropolis are of a nature which would lead any one to the very natural conclusion that we are living in a very barbarous age. The report of this case is thus given by a daily contemporary:-

George Amey, No. 12, Fitzroy-place, was brought before Mr. Knox on a warrant, charging him with having violently assaulted Isabella Amey, his wife.

The wife, who appeared to have been knocked about brutally, said she lived at No. 86, Tottenham-street. Her husband on Saturday week came to her place. He did not live with her but co-habited with another woman, and after a few words began to ill-use her. He knocked her down, jumped on her, and then throwing himself on her, seized her by the throat, and attempted to strangle her. Assistance came in an unexpected form, and she was rescued from further ill-treatment, her husband making his escape.

The wife told the warrant-officer Roskelly that while on the ground and screaming, a favourite cat, named Topsy, suddenly sprang on her husband and fastened her claws in his eyes and her teeth in his face. Her husband could not tear the cat away, and he was obliged to implore her to take the cat from him to save his life.

Mr. Knox, having ascertained that the husband had been in the habit of ill-treating his wife, sent him to prison for one month.

(06.07.1867)

# EXECUTION OF WIGGINS

## FEARFUL STRUGGLE ON THE SCAFFOLD

On Tuesday morning John Wiggins, a lighterman, who was convicted at the last sittings of the Central Criminal Court, of the murder of a young woman named Agnes Oates, with whom he had co-habited in Limehouse, in July last, underwent the punishment of death in front of the gaol at Newgate.

There were probably never fewer people assembled at an execution in London. By seven o'clock and sometime afterwards, the whole length of the Old Bailey from Ludgate Hill, nearly as far as the governor's house, was less crowded than on an ordinary day, and there was no difficulty in reaching the scaffold. This was attributed partly to the then approaching execution of Bordier at Horse-monger-lane gaol, which had the effect, though it would not take place until two hours afterwards, of dividing the crowd. Nor was an assemblage of people collected at an execution ever more orderly perhaps.

The sheriffs (Alderman Stone and Mr. McArthur) with the under-sheriffs, arrived at the prison shortly before eight o'clock. Forming themselves into a procession, with the governor of Newgate, the prison surgeon, the chaplain, and the representatives of the press, they walked to an open yard at the back of the governor's residence. There they halted a few moments, and then the convict attended by two warders, passed before them to the press-room, followed by the authorities.

He was cool and collected and easily submitted himself to the process of pinioning, but complained once or twice that he was being too tightly bound. This process over, the Rev. Mr. Lloyd Jones, the ordinary, addressed a few words of consolation to him, after which the convict said he wished to address the crowd outside. The governor told

him he would not have an opportunity of doing that, and that what he had to say he had better say at once in the presence of the representatives of the press.

The convict then said – "I am entirely innocent of the charge for which I am about to die. I can assure you on my dying oath I never did it. I can go with a clear conscience and a clear heart to my Almighty Maker. It was her that cut my throat and then cut her own. I never lifted a hand or a finger to her, with my dying breath."

With that the prison bell began to toll and the convict was escorted to the scaffold, which he ascended with a light step, attended by the ordinary and the executioner. There a very unusual and a very painful scene occurred. The crowd, on seeing the convict, became very excited, and he began to resist the efforts of Calcraft to place him below the beam. First one of the stalwart prison officers and then another were summoned to assist in restraining him, until four or five of them, with the executioner, were upon the scaffold at the same time.

After the cap had been drawn over his face, the convict shouted to the crowd, "I am innocent: on my dying oath, I am innocent. Cut my head off but don't hang me. I am innocent." By the motion of his lips he began to work the cap off part of his mouth and he continued addressing the crowd, to declare his innocence again and again. Though his arms were pinioned at the elbows, he managed to clutch hold of the rope by which he was about to be suspended, and to hold it for some moments with a firm grasp, swaying himself about, and resisting the attempts of the warders to place him upon the drop, shouting the while that he was innocent. At length he was overcome by sheer force; the rope was adjusted, the drop fell and the convict soon ceased to live. To the last he declared that he was innocent.

Since his trial the convict has availed himself of every opportunity to asseverate his innocence in various terms, and that the woman attempted to cut his throat and then her own. But there is a strong feeling in the public mind, nevertheless, and especially among the prison authorities, that he committed the murder.

On Saturday he was visited by his father, a man upwards of seventy, and during the interview the father repeatedly urged him "to die like man and a Christian." The old man then knelt down, and, in his own simple, homely language, offered up a prayer for his son. The convict had previously seen his brother and his sister-in-law. He was constantly in communication with the ordinary after his conviction, and by the prison authorities was regarded as a man of irascible temper.

On Monday the ordinary had an interview with him and sought to prepare him for death. At times while it lasted the convict was amenable to the exhortations of the rev. gentleman, and at others he rose from his seat and walked about his cell with an air of determination as if it should not contain him.

(19.10.1867)

## DESPERATE ATTEMPT TO RESCUE PRIONERS AT CLERKENWELL

A most desperate and determined attempt to rescue prisoners from custody, during their transit from the Sessions-house to the prison-van was made on Tuesday night by a mob of roughs at Clerkenwell-green.

About half an hour after the court had adjourned for the day, the police made a circle round the door where the prisoners come out. The van was driven up and backed close to the door. A mob of between 200 and 300 persons had collected, and their demeanour was most threatening. The female prisoners who had been convicted during the day, were first removed, and notwithstanding the strong body of police, who were under the direction of an able superior, several of the "roughs" who were of the lowest description, broke through the line, and before they could be prevented nearly succeeded in rescuing a woman, who had been sentenced to a long term of confinement. The police, however, behaved courageously and succeeded in forcing the mob back. No sooner had the line been reformed than a second and more desperate attempt was made. Five roughs succeeded in seizing hold of one of the prisoners, named Alice Turner, who had been convicted of attempting to steal from the person, and had been sentenced to nine months' imprisonment. The police immediately closed with them and a struggle ensued. One of the offenders, who says he is the husband of the woman, struck Warder Crawley in the face, and struggled with him for the release of the

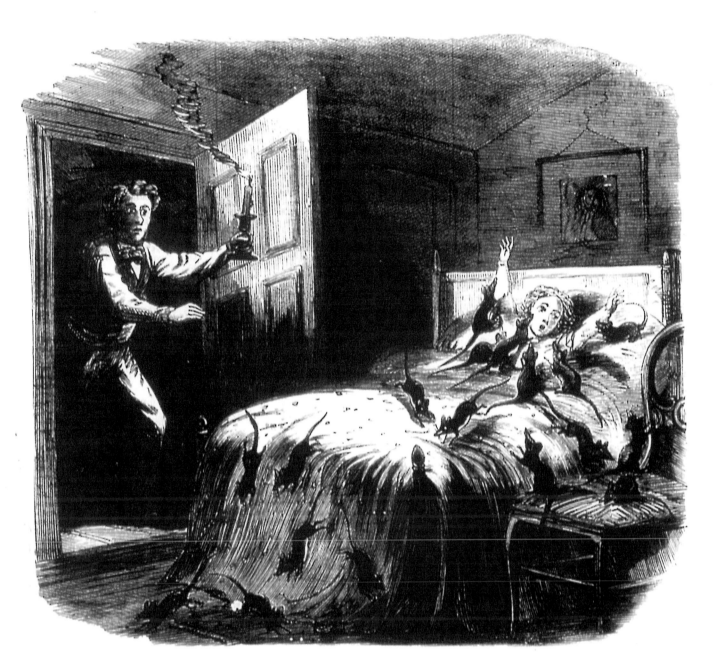

prisoner. She was with some difficulty got into the van, and the door was locked. The roughs finding their efforts fruitless made their escape.

The police, however, succeeded in detaining one of their body, who was with some difficulty conveyed to the station, where he was charged with assaulting the warder and attempting to rescue a prisoner. He was locked up and brought before the magistrate on Wednesday morning.

It is not long since the learned Assistant-Judge, Sir Wm. Henry Bodkin, drew the attention publicly of the authorities to the inadequacy of accommodation for the proper discharge of the duties. Only a few months ago a band of roughs made a set upon the prison-van containing a notorious ruffian named Bodger, who was sentenced to ten years' penal servitude. The officer at that time was struck with brickbats and other missiles, and had the presence of mind to lock the door, and give the key to the officer on duty inside. The scenes occurring daily about this court when the sessions are going forward seriously demand the attention of the proper authorities.

(19.10.1867)

## ATTACKED BY RATS

On Friday evening last week Mr. O'Brien, residing at 27, Wellington-street, was sitting at supper, when piercing cries were heard from the nursery which is on the top floor. Mr. O'Brien hurried to the spot and found the youngest child, a little girl of about fifteen months, had been attacked by several rats. Upon his entering the room with a light they leaped from the bed and escaped. The poor child had been horribly gnawed about the head and arm.

Passing out from the lobby to call his dog which was in the next room, Mr. O'Brien saw a swarm of rats mounting the stairs, not at all daunted by the appearance of the lights. The dog, however, soon put them to flight.

The poor child's arm was much swelled and discoloured. She was at once removed to King's College Hospital. The injury to the arm is regarded by the medical officer as of a very serious character, and it is feared that amputation may be necessary.

(26.10.1867)

## ATTEMPT AT SUICIDE

Jane Townsend, twenty-four, married, was charged at Westminster with attempting to commit suicide by throwing herself into the River Thames.

Michael Hallahan, 155 R, said at half-past nine on Thursday night the prisoner jumped into the Thames opposite Millbank Penitentiary. He took off part of his clothing, and having rescued her, conveyed her in an insensible state to Westminster Hospital where she had remained nineteen hours.

In answer to the usual inquiry, prisoner said she got into a bit of trouble, and jumped into the water to get rid of herself.

The husband of the prisoner, a commissionaire stepped forward, and in reply to Mr. Selfe, said he was very sorry to say his wife was a great drunkard, and had been intoxicated more or less for the last three months. They had been married seven years and had two children, both of whom were now lying at home sick. She had pawned all his things and neglected his home, rendering him so wretched that unless something was

done to reclaim her he felt sure violence would come of it. He had sent his two children away three times, and had to pay 6s. a week for each, but they had been sent home ill; and while he worked hard all day and redeemed what she had pledged, she pawned things again for drink. He wished the magistrate would bind her over to be of good behaviour, and try what effect that would have. She had no trouble except what drunkenness brought her to, and when sober was an exemplary wife.

Prisoner, who seemed to feel her degraded position, said it was, unfortunately, all true. She would promise to take the pledge and reclaim herself.

Mr. Selfe admonished her, and said it was a pity to see a woman with so good a husband degrade herself by the beastly sin of drunkenness. He ordered her to enter into her recognisance of £10 to be of good behaviour for six months, and if she drank again she would be sent to prison.

(16.11.1867)

# CHARGE AGAINST A ROMISH PRIEST

On Thursday, last week, at the Thames Police-court, David Brosnahan, aged forty, a grave-looking man, wearing spectacles, and in the garb of a clergyman, who was described as a Roman Catholic priest, of No 48, Cherry-garden-street, Bermondsey, was charged with indecently assaulting Catherine Moran, a young married woman, dwelling at No.10, Soden-street, Bromley.

CHARGE AGAINST A ROMISH PRIEST

The complainant stated that she was a native of Ireland, and a Roman Catholic. Her husband was fireman at a paraffin manufactory. On Wednesday afternoon she was in her room in the lower part of the house, suckling her child, when the prisoner entered and asked if she had anything for him, which she at once understood to mean did she intend to give him a subscription towards the building of a new Catholic chapel. She said "No, I have not; it is the wrong time of the week." He then took a chair, and sat down opposite to her, and very close to her. She felt a little disconcerted because her dress was open, and her child taking the milk. He then put his hand on her bosom, and she put his hand away. He directly forced his hand on her bosom a second time, and she put it away and arranged her dress. He then asked her to come upstairs, and she told him she would not, and she would tell her husband what he had done. He then left the house and she followed and hallooed and cried.

The first person she saw was a Mrs. Connor, and she told her what the prisoner had done; and Mrs. Connor said; "Never mind him; he came into my house and put his arm around my neck and kissed me; but I took no notice of the thing, owing to the disgrace it would occasion."

In answer to questions by Mr. Benson, the prosecutrix said that she had seen the prisoner once before Wednesday but had not spoken to him. Her daughter, a girl aged seven years, was in the room when he acted as she described. He first asked her if her husband was in. When he asked her to go upstairs he said he would not keep her long.

The Prisoner: I went into her dwelling of course, as I go into a great many persons' houses. I had been to a good number of places on Wednesday.

Mr Benson: I will hear your defence presently. Will you ask her any questions?

The Prisoner: Yes. Did I ask you to go upstairs?

Witness: Yes, twice.

The Prisoner: No. I said, "Is your husband upstairs?"

Witness: You asked me to go upstairs, and said you would not keep me long.

The Prisoner: No; what I said was, "Is your husband upstairs?" Because these people generally live in the upper part of these small houses.

Mrs. Moran was recalled, and said she knew the prisoner was collecting money for a new chapel. He put his hand twice on her naked bosom.

Richard Crone, police-constable, No. 261 R, asked for a remand, and said the prisoner had committed similar offences and taken liberties with women in all parts of London…

Mr. Benson said the case must go to the sessions, and if the prisoner had any witnesses to call to character or otherwise, they would be of value to him. The charge was one of a most serious nature. He committed the prisoner for trial.

(18.09.1869)

*'After deliberating for some time in their box the jury retired to a separate room to consider their verdict. After an absence of about three quarters of an hour they returned with a verdict of not guilty.'* The Times (22.09.1869)

# THROWING A MAN INTO A COPPER OF BOILING WATER

On Friday last at the Lambeth Police-court, Richard Lister, twenty-seven, proprietor of a German sausage manufactory, in James-street, Hatcham, was charged with violently assaulting James Smith and throwing him into a copper of boiling water.

Mr. Ody defended.

225 R said, about quarter before three o'clock in the afternoon he was called in James-street, Hatcham, and was told a man had thrown another into a copper of boiling water. The prisoner opened the door to him, and he asked him what was the matter. He replied "Nothing." He then saw a medical gentleman attending upon an old man named Swift, whose clothes were off and who was wrapped round with bandages. The doctor said the man might die going to the hospital. The injured man said he was picked up bodily by the prisoner, and thrown into the copper of boiling water.

Mr. Edwards, house-surgeon of Guy's Hospital said

## THROWING A MAN INTO A COPPER OF BOILING WATER

Swift was brought into the hospital scalded severely about the face, arms, chest, and back, the skin, in many places being completely destroyed.

Mr. Elliott: Do you consider it a dangerous case?

Mr. Edwards: Most decidedly.

Mr. Elliott: Are there any witnesses to this transaction?

Constable: Two men who saw it were ordered to be here but I cannot find them.

Mr. Elliott: They must be brought here.

After a short adjournment of the case Nathaniel Nottidge was called, and said he worked at the prisoner's factory. He heard the prisoner and Swift quarrelling. Lister struck him with his fist and knocked him down. On Swift getting up prisoner seized hold of him and threw him over his shoulder right into a fifty-five gallon copper, the water in which was about three parts boiling hot.

Mr. Elliott: How is it you did not come here this morning to give evidence?

Police-constable Smith: He was offered money by a person named Langford to go away. Langford was the bail for prisoner.

Mr. Elliott (to witness): Is that so?

Witness: He took me to a public-house, gave me gin and beer and a shilling, and told me I had better go away.

Langford denied the statement.

Witness: It is true, sir; and he said I could have 5s. if I wanted it.

Langford: I lent him the shilling.

Constable: I found the witness in a public-house with Langford and the former told him about the affair.

Mr. Elliott: It is a serious offence; and I order Langford to find bail in £20 to appear at the remand.

Walter Nottidge, another workman at the factory, bore out the evidence as to the assault and the throwing by prisoner of Swift into the copper.

Mr. Elliott ordered a remand.

Mr. Ody applied for bail which was refused.

It will be seen by reference to our police reports that the man has since died.

(23.10.1869)

*At the trial Lister had the opportunity to put his side of the case. The worker Swift was 'the worse for liquor' and had a potato in his hat surrounded by a riband. He boasted that he was an Irish cockney and insulted his boss's wife. Lister warned him; 'Swift don't you talk about my wife.' The final straw was when the drunkard asked his boss for money. Lister was sentenced to nine months with hard labour after suffering extreme provocation.*

# DEATH THROUGH TIGHT-LACING

*Stories from 'New Town' would appear on slow news days and often lacked the specific detail of other reports.*

It would be impossible to form anything like an accurate estimate of the thousands of persons who have fallen victims to the odious fashion of tight-lacing. A melancholy instance of this baneful practice occurred in New Town on Saturday night. Dorothea, the eldest daughter of Vincent Posthelthwaite, Esq. (a highly respectable and wealthy merchant of New Town), died suddenly at a ball given in her father's house. While dancing with a young gentleman to whom she was engaged, she was observed by her partner to turn pale and to gasp spasmodically for breath; she tottered for a few brief seconds, and then fell. The general impression was that she had fainted; restoratives were applied without producing the desired effect. A doctor was sent for, who, upon examining the patient, pronounced the ill fated young lady to be dead.

The consternation of the family and guests may be readily imagined, which was not a little enhanced by the medical gentleman declaring that Miss Posthelwaite had died from no other cause than tight-lacing – the heart's action had been impeded, the excitement and exertion was, under the circumstances, too great a strain upon the system, and hence sudden death.

Our artist furnished us with a picture which is significantly sufficient in itself, without a commentary. Many of our fair readers will be at no loss to divine its meaning, and they will do well by taking a warning therefrom.

(25.06.1870)

## DEATH THROUGH TIGHT LACING

# BABY FARMING

*Margaret Waters was hanged for her callous disregard for children placed in her care in the 'Brixton Baby-Farming Case.'*

We have given in our front page engravings of the poor little emaciated children who have died a lingering death from want of simple nutrient and other causes. The portraits of the miserable little victims may be relied upon as authentic, as they form drawings made from the children themselves. A correspondent furnishes us with the following account of

THE ANTECEDENTS OF THE BRIXTON BABY-FARMERS – ANOTHER DEAD CHILD FOUND.

Important information has been received in reference to the antecedents of Margaret Waters and Sarah Ellis, the two women now in custody charged with neglecting to provide proper food and nourishment for several infants placed under their care. It appears that they have not only been receiving children under a variety of assumed names, but that they have been in the habit of systematically and frequently changing their addresses. Their maiden name is said to be Forth, and their friends to be in good circumstances, residing near Bingley, Leeds, Yorkshire. At present their antecedents in London can only be traced as far back as the second week in February, and it is a remarkable coincidence that dead bodies of children were found at the time in close proximity to the house in which they were residing.

About the 16th of February the prisoners were residing at 15, Bournemouth-road, Peckham. This house they suddenly left, leaving the rent unpaid and tradesmen's bills in the neighbourhood unsettled. From here they are traced to No. 1, Boston-cottages, John-street, Southampton-street, Camberwell; here they only stayed four days and then suddenly left. Next it is ascertained they lived in a house close by Clapham Junction Railway station, where they remained only a week. Their residence is next traced to Lockington-road, York-road, Battersea and from here it is believed they went direct to No. 4. Frederick's-terrace, where their baby farm was discovered, on the 23rd of March.

Whilst the prisoners were residing in Battersea the dead body of a female child was found in St. George's-terrace, Battersea, and on the 15th of March a male infant was found alive in St. George's-road, Battersea. On Sunday morning last the dead body of a child was found in an advanced state of decomposition under a pile of wood near to the house the prisoners resided in at Peckham. This body, which is supposed to have lain there nearly four months, was taken to the Camberwell Workhouse, and an inquest opened on it. On the 24th of February, a male child was found in an old rush basket in Stewart's-lane, Peckham.

Several other women have come forward to endeavour to trace the children they have entrusted to the care of the prisoners. One young woman from the neighbourhood of Lisson-grove is in great anxiety about her child – At the close of evidence given at the Lambeth Police-court she was permitted to see the prisoners. She begged of them to tell her where her baby was, but they treated her in a cool, impudent manner, and the only reply she could get was. "We shan't tell you anything about it."

# BABY FARMING – PORTRAITS OF THE VICTIMS

The prisoners are well educated; in personal appearance they are of a low type, having very narrow foreheads, large heavy lower jaws, and puffed flabby faces, giving them an exceedingly dull appearance.

(09.07.1870)

## DREADFUL TRAGEDY AT CLAPTON

A very painful affair, which has cost two lives, has taken place in Upper Clapton, a young mother of twenty-three, having in a fit of despair thrown her two children into the river and drowned herself afterwards.

It appears that the young woman in question, Eliza Jane Cook, was married to a brickmaker, who some time ago emigrated to Canada. A letter received from him quite recently and bearing date the 16th April, explains the motive for the crime of which she has been guilty.

He stated in the letter that as far as he could see it would take him three years to save money to send for her and the children, and he spoke very despondingly of his prospects, saying that the climate was excessively cold in winter, and too hot in summer, and that whereas England was the place for comfort, Canada was only for work, "and what was the youse of that when no work is to be ad?" He mentioned something about sending 10s., but it would appear no money came.

The unfortunate wife, who lived with her mother and sister at No. 1 Caroline-place, Upper Clapton, became quite distracted when she read the letter, and said that there was no use in trying to live on when there was no prospect of anything turning up. She spoke in such a way that her sister feared she intended to destroy her own life and that of her children, and when she took them out on Thursday evening at five o'clock followed her at a distance – a distance that unhappily proved too great.

Mrs. Cook hurried on with her little girl, aged five, and the little boy, aged two years and a half, in the direction of the River Lea, near the High-bridge. The sister, becoming more and more alarmed, stopped to tell a policeman of her fears, and then she and the officer went on after the mother and the children.

THE TRAGEDY AT CLAPTON

Near the coke oven at Barley's-lane the unhappy woman came to a stand at the bank, and catching up first one and then the other child, flung them both into the river. The boy she flung out far into deep water; the girl being more heavy, she lacked strength to throw to any distance, and the little thing fell into the shallow water near the shore. The wretched mother then leapt in herself determinedly, and sank almost at once.

The sister, it appears, was from afar a witness of this terrible drama. She and the policeman and others ran to the spot, and they were in time to save the little girl, who was in the shallows clinging desperately to the grass at the river's brink. The mother and the little boy had sunk.

Drags were got, and the bodies were recovered after some little delay, but life was quite extinct. Both bodies were taken to the mortuary. The little girl is in no danger.

(20.05.1871)

## A STRANGE BEDFELLOW

At Southwark Police-court William Bowie, twenty-nine, stonemason, residing with his wife at 7, Crosier-street, Lambeth, was charged with being on the premises of Mr. Daniels, printer, Friar-street, Blackfriars road, for an unlawful purpose.

The wife of the latter, an elderly female, said she retired to bed a little before twelve o'clock on Saturday night, leaving her husband at work. About three o'clock she awoke and smelt paper burning, and on turning round she saw a man in bed alongside her, who, she thought, was her husband. She did not disturb him, but at once got up and proceeded downstairs to see if the gas and everything else was safe in the house.

On returning upstairs with a light she perceived the prisoner in her bed, he had his coat on, and believing it was her husband, she roused him and asked him to undress himself, when she, to her horror, found it was not her husband.

She screamed out, and one of her lodgers came down and pulled the prisoner out of bed and it was found that her husband had fallen asleep in the workshop over his work. A constable was called in and the prisoner was given into custody. The prisoner was a perfect stranger to her, and had no right in the house.

In answer to Mr. Benson, witness said that the street door was left on the latch and the other doors were locked and bolted. In the prisoner's pocket was found a latchkey which fitted their lock. The prisoner appeared to be the worse for liquor, and she did not think he intended to steal anything or do any unlawful act.

Professor Thomas, the well-known athlete, said he and his wife lodged in the upper part of the house. They retired to rest about twelve o'clock, and having gone through exercises at a music hall he was very tired, and soon got into a comfortable sleep from which he was aroused about three o'clock by Mrs. Daniels calling out, "There's a man in my bed." He partly dressed himself and went down and entered the landlady's bedroom where he saw the prisoner lying on the bed on his face. He turned him round, and seeing it was not Mr. Daniels he pulled him off the bed and called the prosecutor upstairs.

A STRANGE BEDFELLOW

In answer to the charge the prisoner said he was a journeyman stonemason and worked at the new post-office, St. Martin's-le-Grand. He drank a great deal on Saturday afternoon, and had not the least knowledge of entering the prosecutor's house.

The prisoner's wife, a respectable-looking female, here stepped forward, and said the latch-key found on him belonged to their door, and she gave it her husband on Saturday afternoon. He was then the worse for liquor.

Mr. Benson remarked that it was a very extraordinary case. The prisoner lived in Lambeth, full two miles away, and was found in bed with the prosecutor's wife, with a latchkey unlocking his door. He should adjourn the case to give the constable an opportunity of making further inquiries, and accept bail for the prisoner's appearance. On Wednesday Mr Daniels said he had made inquiries about the prisoner and found him to be a very respectable working man. He believed the prisoner was in the habit of visiting someone in the same street, and had mistaken the house in his drunken state.

Mr. Benson observed that it was a most extraordinary case. However, as nothing was known against the prisoner by the police, he should discharge him, with a caution to keep sober for the future, as drunkenness had got him into this trouble.

(20.05.1871)

# A NOBLE ACT – GALLANT RESCUE

On Friday afternoon as the Heron, Woolwich steamer, just emerged from under London-bridge from the upper side, a middle-aged gentleman who was sitting on the rail smoking a cigar, suddenly fell overboard, and was seen struggling in the water, his head being frequently under.

The steamer was stopped and a lifebuoy thrown over, but he evidently was too much exhausted to reach it. At this moment a powerful looking young man on London-bridge divested himself of his shoes, and without taking off his "wide-awake", mounted the parapet, and dived to the great depth below, and, soon rising to the surface, swam to the rescue of the drowning man, whom he held by the collar of his coat until boats put off to their assistance.

The daring of this act of heroism was greeted with immense cheering, and when the two were conveyed to the Swan Hotel, at the foot of the bridge, an immense crowd followed. The police ascertained that the man who fell overboard was a Mr. Peters, residing at the West-end, who was going to Woolwich on business, and the young man who so promptly dived was J.B. Johnson of the Wellington Baths, Leeds, who had come up to town to contend in the champion swimming match at Hendon, and happened to be passing over the bridge at the time. Fortunately the tide was just on the turn from high water, or Johnson's head, diving from so great a height, might have come in contact with the ground.

(10.06.1871)

# FORTUNE-TELLING IN THE NINETEENTH CENTURY

From the evidence of two married women who were engaged by the police, it appears that on Tuesday last, about twenty minutes past nine in the evening, they went to No. 3. Humer-street, Marylebone, and on entering the house they paid sixpence to a woman who gave them a bone ticket.

One of the females entered a back room and saw the defendant Bryant, who shook hands and inquired about her health. He asked her if she was aware on what errand she came, and on her answering in the affirmative he asked her her age. She told him she was 33 years of age. And she was born on the 21$^{st}$ of July. She told him that she was in a little trouble, and he then commenced reading a tract. She told him she did not want to hear it. He said during the next month there would be a surprise to her; and she said her husband was going into the country, and asked if she would ever see him again. The defendant said in the latter end of July or the beginning of August her husband would come back. The defendant asked her if she had any question to ask him, and she said she had not. He gave her two papers, and said one, entitled "Daily Trials" contained what he was going to read to her.

On Wednesday night, between nine and ten o'clock, Detective sergeant McMath and Constables Webb and Carter of the D division, proceeded to the defendant's house, and on going into the front room on the ground floor they saw 30 to 40 young women sitting in the room. A woman was sitting at a table with a number of bone tickets before her. Webb and Carter went into the room, and McMath stopped in the passage.

As soon as the females, who were waiting in the room, know the detectives, they began to scream, and there was a general rush to the door. They knocked Sergeant McMath down, but five were stopped and their names and addresses taken.

On going into the inner room the detectives there saw the defendant. The wall was covered with pictures relating to the various planets. One picture represented life, death &c., and others represented the nativity of her most gracious Majesty the Queen, the Prince of Wales, the Empress of France, Constance Kent and several others. A medicine chest containing a number of bottles, a quantity of memoranda relating to the nativity of certain people, and a magic mirror, which has a revolving cylinder was in the room. The mirror shows the figures of men and women, old and young.

When the defendant was told he would be taken into custody, he said, "I did tell fortunes, but I am not the principal, Mr. Yundavesta is the principal." A book of fate was also found in the room, and, among other things, a paper which contained the number of visitors every week. The following is a list for several weeks, but they were not dated: - 602, 250, 502, 380, 512, 513, 480, 89, 466, and Good Friday week 217. He was taken to police-station, when he said he was a phrenologist, and was only the servant of Yundavesta.

On the 14$^{th}$ June the females went to the house of the defendant, Shepherd, and paid 6d. to a lad, who gave them a bone ticket, and saw defendant in the back room

HEROIC CONDUCT OF J. B. JOHNSON.

on the ground floor. They went in separately, and he asked one of them if she wanted her fortune told, and on her answering in the affirmative he took a yard tape and measured her head. He said she was born in a lucky month, and she asked him if she was going to be married, and if so who to. He said she would be married to a respectable mechanic, and in answer to her question he said she might have a child, or perhaps two. He asked her if she would have her nativity taken, and she would have more told her. He said it would cost 2s. 6d., and she said she had not got enough money and would call another day. Before leaving he gave them both a circular with their phrenological organs. One was – "Benevolence full, combativeness small, language good, causality small, compassion small, individuality small." The other was "Benevolence full, combativeness small, language small, causality small, compassion small, individuality small."

FORTUNE TELLERS IN TROUBLE.

The defendant has circulated a large number of hills stating he has been to Rome, Palestine, Jerusalem, and the Holy Land, and he can be consulted upon any matter appertaining to travels, absent friends, removals, love, matrimony, children, business speculation &c. On Wednesday night he was taken into custody by inspector Lewis of the D division, and the detectives, and in the room was found a large quantity of letters, some ready to go away and some just broken open, a magic mirror, a large number of photographs; a lawyer's gown was found behind a curtain in the room. Some time ago he was sentenced to two months' imprisonment from the Mansion House for unlawful possession.

On the same evening the females visited the defendant Henry, and they obtained admission to his room under precisely similar circumstances as the

others. He told one of them that she would meet with little trifles, but they would be nothing to speak about. She was born on the rising of the sun, and there was a bright day before her.

Between July and December she would see happiness. She asked if there would be a death in her family, and he said she would have two children before a death. He was taken into custody and a large quantity of papers &c. were found in the room.

The case against the defendant Shipton was exactly the same as the previous cases.

Mr. Pain, for the defendant Bryant, contended that his client had not infringed the law, if he had the Crystal Palace Company ought to be summoned for allowing a magic mirror to be there.

The other defendants said they did not know they were doing any harm.

Mr. Mansfield sentenced each of the defendants to be imprisoned and kept to hard labour in the House of Correction for three calendar months.

(01.07.1871)

# EXTRAORDINARY SUICIDE OF A POLICE SERGEANT

A horrible occurrence took place on Tuesday last week.

For some years a sergeant of the G division of police, named George Brindle, lived with his wife and three children at No. 5, George's-buildings, close to Barbican. The man, who was fifty years of age, had served twenty-four years in the G division, and at the end of his full period of service, which terminated three years ago, he was placed by the police commissioner upon the reserve list, and was granted a pension for the rest of his life of £15 a year.

He then erected at the back of his house, and in the garden, a wooden shed, 16 feet in length and 8 feet in width. The roof of the shed he covered with tiles. He was in the constant habit of locking himself up in the shed for the purpose of doing carpentry work and boot making, by which means he added to his income.

He and his wife lived happily, until about six months ago he became exceedingly jealous of her, making certain unfounded charges against her, and when she denied his accusations he refused to believe her. The disagreements between them on the subject were perpetual, and he ultimately gave way to drink, as he said, to forget all about it.

On Monday evening, at five o'clock, he went into the garden at the back of the house and entered the wooden shed. He was then sober, but he bore a gloomy expression of countenance. After he entered the shed he was heard to fasten it on the inside. In ten minutes afterwards the whole neighbourhood was alarmed by a loud explosion, and upon several persons rushing to see what was the matter, they saw the tiled roof of the shed blown off, and the side of it blown out. There was a strong smell of gunpowder, and when the smoke and dust cleared away Sergeant Brindle, who was a powerful muscular man of six feet two inches in height, was found lying on his back in an unconscious state. He was

EXTRAORDINARY SUICIDE OF A POLICE SERGEANT

frightfully charred and burnt by powder about the chest and face. Some men lifted him off the ground, and having discovered that he was alive his temples were bathed with cold water and he then revived.

The driver of a railway wagon, who was passing by, said, "I will take him to the hospital in my wagon." But Brindle replied in a very cool manner, "Call a cab. I should prefer to go in one." A four-wheeled cab, No. 5,881, was then procured, and the sergeant was lifted into it, and placed sitting on a seat at the back of the vehicle. The cab was then driven along Barbican, in the direction of St. Bartholomew's Hospital. Two young men, one a barman at a public-house, having undertaken to see the deceased to the hospital rode inside the cab with their backs to the horse, and they carefully watched every movement of Brindle.

The cab had not been in motion two minutes before Brindle suddenly thrust his right hand into his trousers pocket and pulled out a razor, which he quickly opened and drew across his throat, inflicting a severe wound upon it. The young men instantly threw themselves upon him, and a struggle, which they describe as fearful, ensued.

The wretched man fought desperately, and threw the young men back on their seat. They rose again and caught hold of his arm, and by a united effort upon their part succeeded in compelling him to let the razor fall into the bottom of the cab. One of the young men then stooped for the purpose of picking the razor up; while he was doing so Brindle pulled a second razor out of his trousers pocket, and he then, to use the words of the barman, "cut into his throat from the left side to the right." He cut the neck two-thirds through, and then his head fell back, exposing to view a horrible gash, from which the blood flowed in great quantities.

The excitement in the street was very great, for the passers-by saw the deceased cutting his throat after he had struggled with the young men, and a crowd of about 800 persons followed the cab to St. Bartholomew's hospital. Brindle upon his arrival there, was found to be dead, and his clothes and the cab were saturated with blood. The surgeons who examined the body state that they never saw so severe a self-inflicted wound upon the throat before.

(19.08.1871)

# HAMPSTEAD SMALLPOX HOSPITAL – STRANGE REVELATIONS

An inquiry as to the management of the Hampstead Hospital, ordered by Government to be held, was opened on Tuesday last week, at the office of the Asylum Board, London. As a great deal has been said in reference to recent proceedings about this hospital, the investigation created much interest…

James Henry Willis, a clerk, said that in February he was admitted to the hospital. Before his arrival they insisted that his name was "Bell." He had a new gown and was tied down by one of the assistants, or by a convalescent patient. He was tied against the sharp edges of the bedstead, as the marks on his legs would show. (Witness then exhibited his legs showing the marks.) There was a most decided insufficiency of beef tea during the night. He had often asked for a drink and been unable to get any, and this occurred to more than himself. Some boiled mutton was handed on a plate which was as cold as ice and a potato was given him that a pig would not touch. His appetite was good; but his food being bad he could not eat it. If the food had been good it was not sufficient to satisfy his cravings. The patients at the end of the ward occasionally did not get their bread. The potatoes were abominably bad, and that from no fault in the cooking.

There were two paid nurses to a ward, in which there were thirty-four beds. If they attended to the patients properly, they could not do their work efficiently. Each convalescent was obliged to make his or her own bed and give what assistance he or she could in the wards. There was only one regular night nurse.

Whilst suffering from erysipelas he was placed in No. 4 ward. At night the nurse would come in, lower the gas and say "good night." The nurse was supposed to look in once or twice during the night, and look after the fires. On one occasion, about the middle of April, a patient was dying, and witness asked a neighbouring patient to fetch the nurse. He went out and before he returned, death had taken place. In ten minutes time the nurse came. She asked for assistance in laying the body out, but the patients refused, as the corpse was in such a bad condition. This was about two a.m. and the body was not removed till five a.m. When the nurse left the room for the night the man was dying. She said, "I don't think that man will live till the morning." As to his lameness, whether it was caused by tying down or the disease he was unable to say, but he knew that he was maimed for life.

John Hunt, the manager of a public-house, said that in March last he had the small-pox, and went into No. 9 ward. Whilst there he was tied down with sheets. The

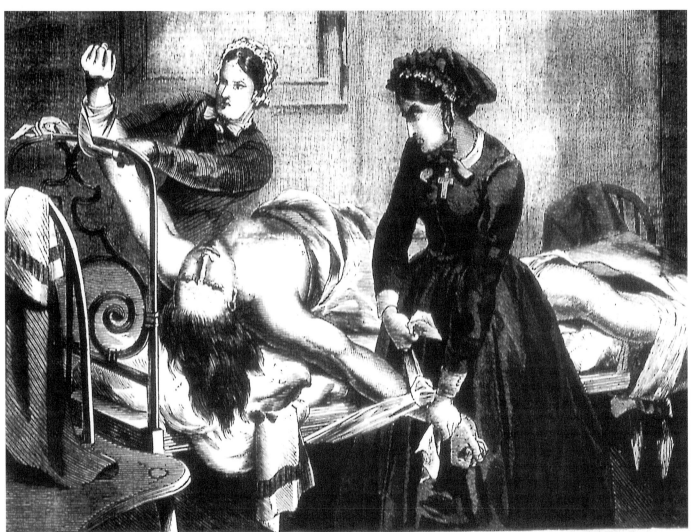

THE HAMPSTEAD HOSPITAL SCANDAL

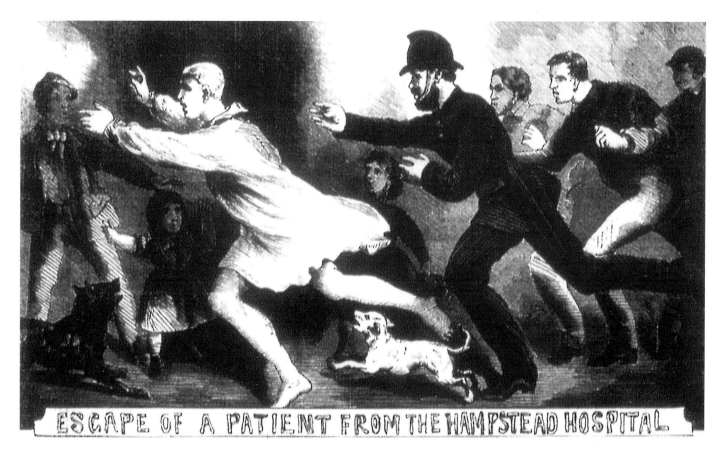

ESCAPE OF A PATIENT FROM THE HAMPSTEAD HOSPITAL

patients complained to one another of the tying. During the night time he often asked for milk, and was often told by the night nurse that she had not got any.

The investigation into the management of the Hampstead Small-pox Hospital was resumed on Monday. Several patients gave evidence as to the practice of tying down delirious persons in bed, but it was stated that this was kept from the knowledge of the surgeons.

John Channon, the first witness, questioned by Mr. Montagu Williams, said: The patients were generally untied from half-past five till six in the morning. The doctors came about ten.

By Dr, Buchanan: During the eight days witness was in the acute ward about twenty patients were delirious. There were not enough nurses to attend to them if there were three or four out of bed at once. He slept more during the day than at night. There was always such a lot of "hollering" at night that he could not sleep. Once saw a doctor in the ward between twelve at night and eight in the morning. He knew one patient made sore by the means used to tie him down. There was a patient who broke loose and tried to get out of the window. He was all over sores, through having torn himself with scratching, and he died at dinner-time on the day after he had tried to get out of the window. That patient had not a strait-waistcoat on. Witness kept watch one night in the fever ward. No nurse or doctor came there all night. Witness had orders to give them their milk and their medicine…

Mr. Albert Emerson Denton, solicitor's clerk, was in the hospital from 3rd May to 15th June, and had seen more than a dozen patients tied down with sheets in No. 10 ward. He described the lavatories and towels in the same way as other witnesses. He corroborated other evidence as to the toughness of the meat, which he said was like leather; the dirtiness of the sheets, and the insufficiency of milk. They were without oil to put on their sores for a whole week. Patients did not get as much spirits as they were ordered by the visiting doctor. The nurses had them completely in their power and patients were punished by them for complaining. One man, named Merrifield, complained of not receiving his proper amount of stimulants, and the nurse had it struck off his card altogether…

The court adjourned.

(30.09.1871)

## AN ASSAULT WITH FLOWER POTS

Agatha Burch was charged with having assaulted a married woman by throwing flower pots on her head. The prosecutrix resided opposite the prisoner's house, and on the previous day a quarrel, which the constable in the case said had lasted for weeks, was commenced between the prisoner and another woman, and one of them threw a stone at the other, which, however, went through a window into prosecutrix's room. She came out demanding to know why her window had been broken, but the prisoner replied by throwing a flower-pot from the window-sill on to the prosecutrix. It struck her on the head, inflicting a severe wound and covering her with blood. Prisoner followed this up by throwing a second flower-pot. Fortunately Police-constable 7 K Reserve came up in time to witness the assault and immediately took the prisoner into custody.

In defence prisoner said the prosecutrix called her by a vile epithet. She had done it in a fit of passion. Mr Hannay sentenced her to a month's imprisonment.

(11.11.1871)

ASSAULT WITH FLOWER POTS

## TWO PRISONERS FLOGGED AT NEWGATE

There was a scene in Newgate on Saturday morning which would, we should think, have an excellent effect on "roughs" and garrotters could they have been witnesses of the exhibition and seen its effect.

At ten o'clock Mr. Sheriff Bennett and Under-Sheriffs Beard and Crossley, arrived with whom were about half a dozen representatives of the press; the Governor, Mr. Jones, and the surgeon. On one side stood a black set of old-looking stocks with holes for wrists, the bottom being an enclosed box. There was no delay; Mr. Sheriff Bennet stood watch in hand; close to him a stoutish, short, grey man, in what is known as a Cardigan jacket, and two warders ushered in the first prisoner, Bernard Regan, a stout, muscular young fellow, with a low type of countenance, guilty of helping to inveigle a man up a court, where the poor wretch was nearly kicked to death, robbed, and left with one eye hanging out upon his cheek.

Bernard Regan had been sentenced to thirty lashes, seven years' penal servitude, and seven years' police supervision. The warders assist him to prepare: There was a good deal of the wild beast about his aspect, but he took all very coolly, and in a few seconds the cross arms of the stocks were opened and closed up on his wrists, and the box like lower part opened, admitting him, and enclosing the lower part of his body.

Now Calcraft steps forward armed with a whip, whose handle is a couple of feet long and whose thongs - nine - are of stout whip-cord.

"Lash."

There is a slight hissing through the air, and the thongs fall with a dull pat upon the naked flesh from the right shoulder diagonally to the waist. The man winces slightly, but bears it without a murmur.

Lash! lash! lash! slowly and regularly, and after the first three or four, thin red lines streaks the prisoner's back, but no blood. The lashes fall on slowly and regularly, but no cry escapes the man till the twelfth, when he begins to writhe a little, and utters a suppressed "Oh!" The skin now grows furiously red, and the lines streaked across run one into the other till by the time twenty lashes had been administered a broad scarlet band, like a heraldic bar sinister, marked the ruffian who now uttered a dull "Oh!" half sigh, half groan, - at every blow – blows administered with the greatest coolness by Calcraft.

"Flog fairly," exclaimed the prisoner, at last, evidently asking for a distribution of the lashes over a wider surface; but they fell in the same line regularly and methodically to the thirtieth, when the man was cast loose, the blood ready to start through the bruised skin, but not a strand of the cat stained, and the man merely looking a little faint as he walked back to his cell. The time of execution was but one minute and twenty seconds.

Samuel Lilley was the second offender upon whom sentence was to be carried out; a younger, more boyish-looking fellow. He stood smiling as he stripped off his shirt, evidently holding the preparation in contempt, but his thinner, fairer skin threatened to give place to more suffering, as it proved.

His punishment was to be but twenty-five lashes for robbery with violence, and the same term of imprisonment and supervision awarded to his fellow. A minute sufficed for him to be secured in position, and the flogging recommenced.

TWO RUFFIANS FLOGGED IN NEWGATE

A TELL TALE PARROT-THE DISCOVERY

The first blow made the poor wretch wince terribly, writhing, as far as his well-secured arms and legs would allow. Suppressed exclamations escaped him as the blows fell, and it seemed as if involuntarily the quivering muscles crept closer to the stock, so as to place a few more inches distance between them and the executioner, the man curving his back inwardly, and twisting himself about so as to hinder the strokes of Calcraft, who stopped, and drew the lashes through his left hand from time to time, disentangling them, and waiting till the man resumed his upright attitude before he continued the flogging.

"Don't stop, please!" "Keep on, please!" the prisoner exclaimed, as the halts were made, and then another and another blow fell, Calcraft coolly telling the writhing culprit to hold still, or he would only hurt himself all the more.

"Don't stop, please; bit further up, please," were the next appeals, and at last in his agony the man laid his head down upon one arm with a gasping utterance – that peculiar sibilant drawing in of the breath of one in intense pain. The affects were the same as in the last; the diagonal pink lines growing scarlet, and running one into another till there was a broad scarlet band, which quivered and flushed and changed colour. But there was no blood.

Twenty-four, twenty-five, lashes fell, and then a loud voice cried, "Stop!" and the prisoner was cast loose, to walk quietly away from the post. There had been no shrieks or loud groans – nothing to indicate that the punishment was very terrible. No appearance of fainting, nothing more than might be expected from a sharp lashing that tingled and burned the skin to a tremendous extent, no doubt. There was nothing in fact, more than what was deemed to be wholesome punishment. That it was deserved, the amount given of the misdeeds fully bears out.

(25.11.1871)

## A TELL-TALE PARROT – NO FOLLOWERS ALLOWED

We are indebted to the *South London Press* for the following account of an interesting little domestic drama, a leading incident of which will be found depicted in our front page:-

"An old maiden lady recently engaged a cook on the express understanding that no 'followers' were to be allowed. Matters went on smoothly enough until Saturday evening last, when the old lady in question unexpectedly intruded herself into the cook's domain.

On entering she was greeted by the shrill scream of a loquacious parrot which had been doomed to penal servitude in the kitchen on account of the bad habit he had of making unearthly noises. The old lady put her fingers into her ears – and it would have been well had she kept them there; for the moment she withdrew them, Poll muttered, in sepulchral tones, 'He kissed cook.'

These words, to the apparent discomfiture of cook, immediately attracted the attention of the old maid – such impropriety indeed – no wonder! 'What?' she exclaimed, gazing eagerly upon the bird. 'Under dresser' replied Poll, in the same husky voice.

Notwithstanding cook's protestations that rats had been heard under said dresser, the mistress insisted on an investigation. There was no help for it; the table-leaf was raised, when, lo! The astonished mistress there discovered concealed a full blown – not a policeman, but a guardsman booted and spurted. 'My cousin, ma'am.' said the blushing cook; but the explanation apparently was not considered satisfactory, as the old lady is advertising, with this addendum – none need apply under forty-five!"

(06.04.1872)

A POLICEMAN ASSAULTING HIS SERGEANT

# A DRUNKEN POLICEMAN ASSAULTING HIS SERGEANT

William Kitchen, a constable of the C division, was charged with being drunk while on duty and assaulting Sergeant Wells, 15 C. At a quarter-past two o'clock on the morning of the 28th, Sergeant Wells, 15 C, while on duty in Hay-hill, Berkely-square, saw the prisoner who was also on duty, run down Bruton-mews, evidently trying to avoid him. The sergeant went after the prisoner and found him to be drunk, and ordered him to the station.

As the prisoner refused to do so the sergeant told some constables to take him there, and assisted in doing so, when the prisoner threw him and struck him three times, and behaved with great violence, and when at length, and with considerable difficulty, he was got to the station, he made an ineffectual attempt to strike the inspector (Mr. Browning).

Superintendent Dunlop having spoken unfavourably of the prisoner's conduct as a constable, Mr. Knox said he considered the case a bad one, and any fine he could impose would be inadequate to meet it, and, therefore, committed the prisoner (who had only a few hours longer to remain in the force) for a month, with hard labour.

(11.05.1872)

# AN ARTFUL MONKEY

At the Greenwich Police-court a few days since, a respectably dressed man presented himself, and asked the assistance of Mr. Maude under peculiar circumstances.

He stated that he resides at Sydenham in a house adjoining which a person is keeping a large-sized, old and artful monkey, which, he understood, gained a first prize at a recent show of monkeys held at North Woolwich Gardens. The monkey was kept in a garden, having a chain and a strap, the latter of which he contrived to unfasten, and thus getting loose, had pursued his (the applicant's) wife, who had to jump over a fence to avoid it. He had spoken to the owner of the monkey, from whom he could get no satisfaction, and neither his wife nor his family was safe. He thought the owner of such an animal should be compelled to cage it.

Mr. Maude said he was afraid he could not render the applicant any assistance, as he had not the power of the Court of Chancery to grant an injunction against the owner. Neither could he issue a warrant for the monkey's apprehension, its trespassing not being in a public thoroughfare. The applicant's only remedy would be in a civil not in a criminal court of law.

(24.08.1872)

AN ARTFUL MONKEY, MY NEXT DOOR NEIGHBOUR

## STRANGE SPIRITUAL MANIFESTATION

*This story about strange apparitions was one of many reprinted in the IPN from other newspapers. In this case we join a reporter from the Daily Telegraph.*

Miss Blank's papa – for the lady is but sixteen – lives on the outskirts of London, as spiritualists always seem to do; and is a respectable man in some commercial line of life. Beside the medium, who is a pretty Jewish-like little girl, there were three other children present, all of whom discoursed on spirits in the most off-hand way. Mamma and Aunt made up the domestic portion of our circle, and there were, besides, the editor of a spiritualist journal, another pronounced Spiritualist, a doctor from the country, who had had something to do with developing the medium, and had been converted by her to the doctrines of Spiritualism, an old gentleman, from Manchester, and myself – eleven in all, irrespective of our little hostess, the pretty medium.

After a brief confab in the front parlour, we descended to the nether regions where the spirits were in the habit of making their appearance in a small breakfast-room next to the kitchen. The original method of "development" was simple in the extreme. Miss Blank went into the room alone. A curtain was stretched across the open doorway, leaving the aperture of about a foot deep; and in this rather Punch-and-Judy like opening, portions of the spirit face gradually showed themselves – first a nose, then an ear, &c. – to the circle who sat on the stairs.

Now, however, that the power was more developed, a sort of corner cupboard had been fitted up with two doors opening in the usual manner from the centre, and an aperture of some eighteen inches square in the fixed portion at the top. At this I was told the faces would appear. A lamp on a table in the other corner of the room was so arranged as to shed a bright light on this opening, whilst it left the rest of the small apartment in subdued but still in full light. I examined the cupboard or cabinet carefully, put a chair in, and saw little Miss Blank carefully shut up inside like a pot of jam or a pound of candles. A rope was put in her lap, the object of which will appear anon, and we all sat round like a party of grown-up children waiting for the magic lantern.

We were told to sing, and so we did – at least the rest did; for the songs were Spiritualistic ones for the most part, which I did not know. They were pretty cheerful little hymns, such as "Hand in hand with Angels," "The Beautiful River," and Longfellow's "Footsteps of Angels." By-and-bye raps inside the cupboard-door told us to "open sesame." We did so; and there was pretty Miss Blank tied round the neck, arms, and legs, to the chair, in a very uncomfortable and apparently secure manner. We sealed the knots, shut her up in the cupboard, and warbled again.

After some delay a face rose gently to the aperture, rather far back, but presently came well to the front. It was slightly pale, and the head was swathed in white drapery. The eyes were fixed and altogether it looked ghostly. It remained for some time, disappeared and re-appeared; and the lamp was turned full upon it, but the eyes never lost their fixed stare, and showed no symptom of winking. After several minutes it went altogether. The doors were opened, and little Miss Blank was found, still tied, with seals unbroken, and to all appearance in a deep sleep. Miss Blank was awakened, uncorded, and taken to walk for a quarter of an hour in the back garden, as she was much exhausted; and we went upstairs to recruit as well. We had to make this break twice during the evening.

When we reassembled after a good deal more singing than I cared about, another appearance took place in obedience to the command of the doctor who had been in the East and asked to see a Parsee friend. After some delay a head appeared, surrounded by a turban, and with a decidedly Eastern expression of countenance and dark complexion. This was tableau No. 2, which took a long time, and almost interminable singing to bring about.

There was another adjournment. The children were sent to bed, and the maid-servant – who it appeared, was great at singing – came in from the kitchen to join the circle. There was an advantage, mamma and papa told me, about these manifestations; they rendered their children quite superior to all ideas about the "Bogey." I could not help asking myself whether I should have dared to go to bed under such circumstances in my days of immaturity.

In Scene the Third, the face was quite different. The head was still surmounted by white drapery, but a black band was over the forehead, like a nun's hood. The teeth were projecting, and the expression of the face sad. They fancied it was a spirit that was pained at not being recognised. When this face disappeared, Katie came again for a little while, and allowed me to go up to the cupboard and touch her face and hand, after first putting to me the pertinent question, "Do you squeeze?" On assuring her I did not do anything so improper, the manipulations were permitted. This was the finale, and the circle broke up forthwith. The gentleman from Manchester was delighted, and all the Spiritualists, of course, were loud in their comments.

I reserved my judgement, as my custom always is when I see anything that beats me.

(19.10.1872)

KILLED BY A COFFIN AT KENSAL GREEN CEMETERY

## KILLED BY A COFFIN

Dr. Lankester held an inquest at the University College Hospital on the body of Henry Taylor, aged twenty-six. The evidence of Mr. E.J.Reading, an undertaker's foreman, and others, showed that on 19th instant deceased, with others, was engaged at a funeral at Kensal-green cemetery.

The church service having been finished, the coffin and mourners proceeded in coaches towards the place of burial. The day being damp, the foreman directed the coaches with the mourners to proceed to the grave by the footway, and the hearse across the grass towards a grave-digger, who was motioning the nearest way.

The coffin was moved from the hearse and being carried down a path only three feet by six wide, by six bearers, when orders were given to turn, so that the coffin, which was what is known in the trade as a 4lb. leaden one, should go head first.

While the men were changing, it is supposed that deceased caught his foot against a side stone and stumbled; the other bearers, to save themselves, let the coffin go, and it fell with great force on to deceased, fracturing his jaw and ribs.

The greatest confusion was created amongst the mourners who witnessed the accident, and the widow of the person about to be buried nearly went into hysteria. Further assistance having been procured, the burial service was proceeded with, while deceased was conveyed to a surgery, and ultimately to the above-mentioned hospital, where he expired on the 24th instant.

The jury recommended that straps should be placed round coffins, which would tend to prevent such accidents. Verdict – accidental death.

(09.11.1872)

## THE LENNIE MUTINEERS

*During the mutiny en route to the U.S.A. the captain and first and second mates were thrown overboard. The mutineers wanted to sail the ship to Greece and sell it. This report is from 'The Times' May 24th 1876. IPN report illegible.*

Yesterday morning the four men – chiefly, if not all Greeks – convicted at the last sessions of the Central Criminal Court, before Mr. Justice Brett, and sentenced to death for the part they took in the mutiny and murders on board the Lennie, were executed within the prison of Newgate. Their names, as may be remembered, were Matteo Corgalis, aged 36, better known as "French Peter," Pascaler Caladis, 33, otherwise "Big Harry;" George Kaida, 22, otherwise "Lips;" and Giovanni Cacaria, 21, otherwise "Joe the Cook."

After their trial and conviction the doomed men were repeatedly visited in prison by the Greek Archimandrite in the City of London, Dr. Hieronymous Myriantheus, and by the Greek Vice-Consul M. Lascaridi. Eventually after the brief interval after conviction began to wear away, the convicts are said to have in effect acknowledged their guilt and the justice of their sentence, adding that they must have been tempted by the devil: that they deeply repented the crimes they had committed, and were grateful for the time allowed them for repentance.

After the visits of the Greek Archimandrite they gave themselves up to fasting and prayer, and before retiring to rest on Monday evening they expressed their grateful acknowledgements for the considerate attention and consolation they had received after their conviction from the Greek Archimandrite and the Vice-Consul; "French Peter" adding, it is understood, that in their own country, for such a crime, they would have been executed at once, without any interval for repentance.

The sentence was executed shortly after eight o'clock yesterday morning, in a yard at the back of the prison, the same in which the convict Wainwright was executed, and in like circumstances as to the manner of execution. Besides the representatives of the Press, a limited number of persons were present, as was also a small attachment of the City Police under the control of Superintendent Foster. The Greek Archimandrite accompanied by the Vice Consul, had, it is understood, earlier in the morning visited the convicts in their separate cells, and the Archimandrite had engaged them in prayer. Shortly before eight o'clock the men were introduced to Marwood, the executioner, and submitted themselves to the process of pinioning. They had previously written letters to their friends, which they entrusted to the Greek Consul to be forwarded to their relative destinations.

At length - all the necessary arrangements having been completed – the convicts were seen emerging one by one from the gaol to the place of execution, the prison bell tolling the while, and the Greek Archimandrite attending and sustaining them to the last. First came "French Peter," as he was called; next Claudis, otherwise "Big Harry;" then Kaida, otherwise "Lips;" and lastly Cacaris, alias "Joe the Cook," each wearing a white calico cap.

"Big Harry," on being placed on the scaffold, said, "Good bye, good bye." "Joe the Cook," who had but recently attained his 21st year, appeared to realize the doom that awaited him far more acutely than any of the rest, and as the noose was being adjusted seemed to be on the point of fainting.

At last, all things being in readiness, at a touch by the executioner, Marwood, the drop fell with a dreadful crash, and the men, all of whom were still in their prime, had expiated their crime with their lives. According to the custom of late years, immediately after the sentence of the law had been carried into effect, a black flag was hoisted over the roof of the prison, and the bodies of the convicts, after hanging an hour, were taken down and subsequently submitted to a coroner's inquest, at the conclusion of which, Mr. Gibson, the prison surgeon, having officially certified that life in each case was extinct, a verdict was given in accordance with the circumstances. Later in the day the dead bodies, placed in a shell with quick-lime, were buried within the precincts of the prison – the place of sepulture being part of the sentence – and in immediate contiguity, as it happened, to the remains of the famous Cato-street conspirators.

(27.05.1876)

FRENCH PETER    BIG HARRY    GEORGE KAIDA OR LIPS    JOE THE COOK

EXECUTION OF THE LENNIE MUTINEERS

## A FEMALE SAILOR

Female sailors, says the *Daily Telegraph*, are by no means uncommon phenomena in the history of human eccentricity…But what could have induced the young lady of "considerable personal attractions" who the other day appeared before the sitting magistrate at the Thames Police-court, to assume the jacket, jersey, and other apparel of a forecastle hand?

It seems that the interesting female mariner belongs to a respectable family residing near Dublin. When she was only seventeen, it occurred to her to emigrate – but in proper feminine garb – to Queensland. She obtained a situation as barmaid at an hotel, but soon afterwards received a letter from her mother requesting her to return home, and enclosing the necessary passage-money.

Instead of returning in an undemonstrative manner and the habit of her sex, she purchased a complete equipment of masculine attire, and obtained a berth as second steward on board a steamer plying between Newcastle and Sydney. After two or three months' undetected enjoyment of life on the ocean wave, she thought that she might as well return to Old Ireland, and work her passage as a hand before the mast; so she sought and obtained a berth on the good ship "Strathdon" bound for the port of London.

She behaved herself uncommonly well, and became a general favourite among her shipmates, but a casualty revealed the fact that the popular forecastle hand belonged to the gentler sex and the gallant commander of the "Strathdon," Captain Batho, while "very much applauding what she'd done," caused some female clothing to be procured for her, gave her a cabin, and behaved to her in every way as a sailor and gentleman should do.

A FEMALE SAILOR.

Commendably jealous of the fair fame of the "Strathdon" the hospitable skipper wished the young lady to make a statutory declaration before the magistrate as to how she came on board his vessel; but Mr. Lushington did not think it was necessary for such a course to be adopted.

We are glad to learn that the owners of the "Strathdon" have kindly undertaken to send the fascinating tar home to her parents; and it is to be hoped that she will take the earliest opportunity of espousing an eligible master mariner, when she can occasionally enjoy her penchant for the sea, without being at the pains of running away or disguising herself in male attire.

(27.07.1878)

## EXTRAORDINARY CASE OF SETTING FIRE TO A WIFE AT LOWER NORWOOD – LYNCH LAW

One of the most extraordinary cases of lynch law which has ever taken place occurred some short time since at Lower Norwood, a popular district about eight miles south of London.

Upper Norwood is inhabited by wealthy and respectable people but several parts of Lower Norwood are tenanted by a class of roughs scarcely to be matched in the vilest London slums. It was by some of this class that the outrage of which our illustration this week is given was perpetrated. Though it reads more like a crime which would have been more likely to have taken place among some of the half-civilised parts of America than in a civilised suburb so near to the metropolis, yet the statement is strictly true and in no way exaggerated.

It appears that a little more than a week ago a Mrs. Kensington, the wife of a labourer residing at Lower Norwood, eloped with a rag and bone collector residing in the same locality. The husband of the runaway wife, after she had been absent about four days, traced the truant pair to some lodgings near Lordship-lane, Dulwich.

When they were discovered the rag and bone collector scampered off back to his own wife and children, and the husband took possession of his faithless spouse. She at first was very reluctant to accompany him back, but after a few drops of gin she consented to return to her home.

The husband however seems to have resolved quietly in his own mind to make an example of her. For this purpose he treated her at various houses to a few more drops of the needful, till she was sufficiently jolly and courageous to accompany him anywhere. Having got her into this tractable condition, he coaxed her on till he got her in front of the house where her rag and bone lover lived. Here he at once threw off the mask of protection,

and, renouncing all his wife's past claims upon him, he called to the knight of the rags and bones to admit her to his castle, and take charge of her for life.

The wife of the rag and bone man now came on the scene, and in strong terms rated the false vixen for decoying her man away. By a preconcerted plan, an effigy of the adulterous woman was suddenly bought out; the tin-kettle band at once sounded to arms, and the thumping of the rough music, like the beating of the tom-tom in a wild Indian camp, brought hundreds of savages to the spot.

Shrieks of fury, more hideous than the screams in an Indian war dance, were now raised against the woman taken in adultery, and cries of "Lynch her, lynch her!" went round on every band. Suddenly a number of roughs of both sexes began to pelt her with mud and refuse.

An effigy of her was then brought out, composed of a mast, dressed up as an adulterous guy. Then a large fire was kindled, and the effigy was thrown on the top. While this fire was burning cries were raised of "Set fire to her, too," and the woman was then actually pushed into the fire, and her clothes caught the flames. After this she was

HORRIBLE BRUTALITY—ATTEMPTED LYNCH LAW—LOWER NORWOOD

seized and the whole of her clothing, excepting her chemise, boots and stockings, was dragged from her, and tore nearly to shreds. In this semi-nude state she was actually pushed by some of the worst of the roughs towards the flames again.

Her cries of murder, and entreaties for help were now pitiable, and at last some police arrived upon the scene. They arrived just in time, it is believed, to stop the woman being burned to death.

(05.10.1878)

## THE FIRST SUICIDE FROM FREE WATERLOO BRIDGE

The first suicide from the free Waterloo Bridge took place last week. Mr. Alfred Willeson, aged thirty-one years, lately residing at Boundary-road, St. John's-wood was seen by the police wandering about the bridge. He afterwards sat down on one of the recesses of the bridge where he divested himself of his coat and hat and climbed on the parapet, from which he leaped into the Thames and was drowned.

(19.10.1878)

## THE MYSTERY OF THE HAUNTED KITCHEN REVEALED

*Another 'Newtown' story.*

A strange story reaches us from Newtown. It appears that for some days past most extraordinary noises have been heard in the kitchen of a tradesman's house in the town. The cook and housemaid were seriously alarmed being under the impression that the house was haunted and nothing could persuade them to the contrary.

Eventually the boards of the kitchen were removed by a carpenter, when, to the surprise of all the occupants of the house, a wretched, emaciated-looking man was discovered in almost a dying condition in a vault beneath the kitchen. The poor fellow appeared to be on the verge of starvation, and would certainly have died had he not been discovered in the extraordinary manner already described.

He has been rescued from his prison-house, and is now under the doctor's hands. At present it has not transpired how he got into the vault.

(19.04.1879)

THE MYSTERY OF THE HAUNTED KITCHEN REVEALED

## THE GREAT WALKING MATCH – AGRICULTURAL HALL

Shortly after eight o'clock on Sunday night the six days' competition at the Agricultural Hall came to an end and resulted in another 'best performance on record.' The attendance of spectators was very large all through, and on Saturday the hall was thronged. It would be a matter of some difficulty to do more than guess at the number of people present at the finish, but 20,000 will be well within the mark.

The race had for some time been reduced to a match between O'Leary and Vaughan. Still O'Leary had to walk with great care to avoid a break-down; while Vaughan, on Saturday afternoon and evening, walked and ran with surprising freshness. It is to be regretted that scrupulous impartiality should not have been dealt out to all the men engaged as there is no doubt that when people speak of O'Leary's triumph it will be remembered against him that his entry was at least informal, that he was greatly favoured in having one track to himself, while the other seventeen competitors had to crowd along on the other, and that, while a commodious, comfortable tent was provided for him, the Englishmen were penned up in close huts…

O'Leary maintained one steady pace throughout the day of close upon four miles an hour and gradually increased his lead, eventually winning by 20 miles…

At last at half-past eight the mob broke through the barriers, and all was over. The band played 'God Save the Queen' vigorously as a hint to go, while the police gave the still broader hint of turning out the gas. At last the huge multitude was dispersed and the great walking match was over.

O'Leary walked 117 miles on his first day, 83 on his second, 88 on his third, 86 on his fourth, 83 on his fifth and 86 on his sixth and last day. O'Leary is thirty-two years old and is a naturalised American, weighs 10st. 6lb and is 5ft 8ins. He is a most temperate man, never taking spirits, and as a rule one pint of ale only in ordinary times, but none whatsoever when walking a match.

(03.05.1879)

## THE GIRLS' HOME SCANDAL AT DEPTFORD

At the Central Criminal court on Wednesday, before Baron Pollock, Laura Julia Addiscott, spinster, was placed at the bar to take her trial for the manslaughter of four children placed under her charge in an institution called "The Home for Friendless Girls," at Deptford. The prisoner pleaded "Not Guilty" to all the charges. She was put upon her trial for the manslaughter of a child named Kate Smith. Mr. Besley opened the case for the prosecution.

Sarah Eveleigh, the nurse at the Greenwich Union, said that on the 22nd of April ten children were brought from the home, the sister of the deceased being one of them. They were all in a wretched condition, suffering from Itch, and covered with vermin. Some of the children had been sent from the union, and at that time they were healthy.

THE DEPTFORD "HOME" SCANDAL.

MISS ADDISCOTT. (SKETCHED IN COURT)

Mr. Pilcher, the relieving officer of the union, proved that in consequence of information he received he went to the prisoner's house on the 20th of November, with the medical officer and Inspector Phillips. The prisoner refused to admit them on the first occasion, but he afterwards went over the house.

There was little or no furniture in the house, and the bedding of the children consisted of straw wrapped up in cloth. There was no appearances of food or sanitary arrangements, and a hole in the garden appeared to have been used for sanitary purposes. The fireplaces had soot in them, and did not seem to have any fire in them. It was in November that he visited the house. There were seven children in the house, and in consequence of the state they were in he ordered them to be removed to the union workhouse.

Ellen Smith, a girl thirteen years old, the sister of the deceased, was then examined. She said her father was dead, and she remembered being sent to the union and subsequently to the home kept by the prisoner. Her sister

MISS ADDISCOTT'S "HOME FOR FRIENDLESS GIRLS".

was a year younger and she went with her. The prisoner told her that she was fifteen years old, and too old to go to school, and she wanted her at home. Four of the girls were sent out every day with collecting cards, and they generally bought home about 5s.. She described their food as sopped bread and treacle for breakfast, and boiled oatmeal for dinner. They had nothing more till ten at night, when they had oatmeal again, and sometimes bread and treacle. Sometimes they had meat on Sundays, small pieces that were bought by the prisoner on Saturday night.

She went on to say that she remembered one of the children, Alice Maud Edgar, dying, and another child, a baby, named Kate Birch. They were both very weak before they died. All the children, she said, suffered from cold, and there was no fire in any of the rooms except the kitchen. Witness and three other children used to sleep in their clothes, and they had no blankets or counterpanes, and at this time there was only one blanket in the house.

GIVING THE GIRLS THEIR SUPPER.

The witness said she remembered her sister dying on the 6th of April. She was covered with vermin, and the prisoner told her to wipe them off and throw them into the fire, and a fire was lighted for the purpose. Witness's stepfather came to the house while her sister was lying dead, and the prisoner refused to allow him to see her, but did not say that she was dead. She said that at the time she died her sister's bones were coming through her skin, and the prisoner told her to pick off the vermin before the undertaker came to put her in the coffin.

On one occasion shortly before her death the prisoner beat her sister with a cane. She also once struck witness because she accidentally upset a cup of coffee, and the prisoner said that if any of them kept her from going to church on the Sunday they should never see another Sunday. She said that she had also seen the prisoner beat the baby, Kate Birch, and she observed marks on her body after she was dead.

Elizabeth Maria Edgar, a child eleven years old, who had been two years in the home, was then examined.

She said that she was hungry almost every day while she was in the home, and she also suffered from cold. She corroborated the evidence given by the girl, Ellen Smith, with regard to the food that was supplied to them. She also said that the prisoner used to beat her frequently with a clothes line....

Mr. Grain addressed the jury for the defence, and he endeavoured to show that the prisoner had done all that was in her power, having regard to her means, for the children, and that the death was more probably owing to the diseased condition of these poor children than to any wilful or criminal neglect on the part of the prisoner.

A number of witnesses were called for the purpose of showing that the prisoner had purchased coals, bread, and other necessaries for the home in considerable quantities, and also that persons who had seen the children on several occasions did not observe anything wrong in their appearance. Several members of the prisoner's family were examined, and they stated that the children had plenty of food, and were properly treated, and they contradicted the evidence given by the children in many particulars.

Dr. Ayers, a medical gentleman practising at Deptford, proved that he had attended the deceased, and he considered her a scrofulous subject, and that this disease was the cause of death. He also denied that there were any vermin on the body at the time of the death.

The jury found the prisoner "Not guilty." They at the same time said they were of opinion that institutions of this description uninspected were calculated to lead to great abuse. Baron Pollock said he thought this was a very proper rider to the verdict, and he would take care that it was conveyed to the proper quarter.

Mr. Besley intimated that it might be considered advisable to proceed with one of the other indictments, and the matter would be considered between this and the next session. In the meantime the prisoner was admitted to bail.

(16.08.1879)

## THE EXECUTION OF CATHERINE WEBSTER AT WANDSWORTH

At nine o'clock this morning Catherine Webster was executed in Wandsworth Gaol for the murder of Mrs. Thomas at Richmond. The proceedings were strictly private, owing to the decision of the Sheriffs of the county not to admit representatives of the press. Nevertheless some facts concerning the convict transpired amongst the crowd which had collected outside.

It seems that Webster, after making a short confession late on Monday night, to the effect that she alone committed the deed, told Father McEnnery, the Roman Catholic Chaplain, that she felt relieved at having unburdened her conscience, and that she would sleep more calmly on that her last night on earth than she had done since her condemnation.

THE NIGHT BEFORE T

THE MURDER

THE DREAM OF KATE WEBSTER

She retired to rest soon after ten and slept fairly well. She arose soon after five this morning and was at once visited by the Governor of the prison, Captain Colville, whose kindness to her since she has been under his care the convict has spoken highly of. At 7.30. a.m. Father McEnnery arrived, and he was followed very quickly by the surgeon of the gaol. Marwood had slept on the premises, and was up betimes, making all the final preparations for carrying out the law. At 8.30 the Under Sheriff for Surrey, Mr. Abbott, arrived, and soon after the process of pinioning was gone through. Just before nine the procession started for the scaffold,

Father McEnnery reading the burial service. The prison bell commenced tolling at a quarter to nine, and at three minutes past that hour, the black flag was hoisted on the flagstaff, denoting that Catherine Webster was no more. The appearance of the flag was greeted with some cheering by the crowd.

(02.08.1879)

*Kate Webster was possibly the most hated and cold-blooded murderess of the nineteenth century. Following*

her dismissal as a servant to a Mrs. Julia Thomas she wreaked a most horrendous revenge. As her employer returned from Sunday service, Kate leapt out at her wielding an axe, which, following a struggle, was embedded in Mrs. Thomas's skull.

There was no doubt as to the premeditation of the crime as the servant had begun boiling a large pot of water long before the return of her mistress. Kate methodically sliced up the body and immersed it in the boiling water. The following day the par-boiled remains and bones were placed on a large fire in the kitchen. Some of the remaining body fat was offered for sale as 'best dripping' by the callous char who took to wearing her mistress's clothes and pawning her jewellery for drink.

What remained of the body was jammed into a box and thrown off Richmond Bridge.

Arrested in Ireland, Kate Webster was found guilty after a seven-day trial. According to reports released after that of the IPN, Kate Webster showed no remorse on the gallows and 'broke out into the most appalling language.'

KATE WEBSTER

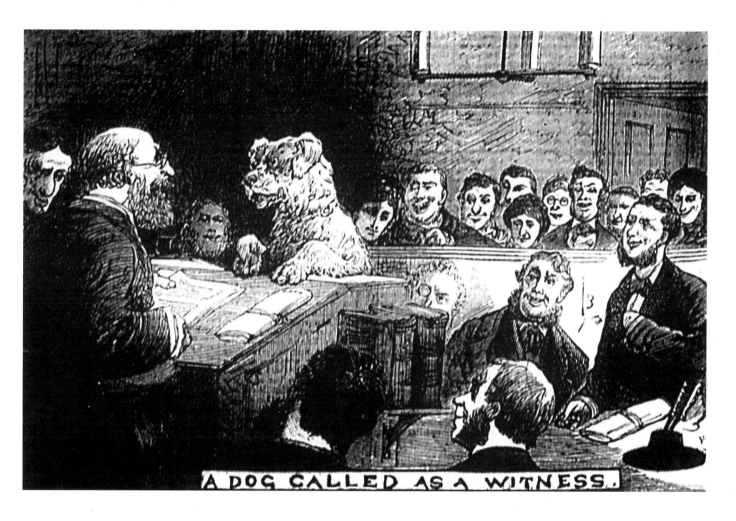

A DOG CALLED AS A WITNESS.

## A DOG CALLED AS A WITNESS

At the Hammersmith Police-court, Mr. Theodore Gordon, of Godolphin-road, Shepherd's-bush, was summoned by Frederick William Hoare for allowing a ferocious dog to be at large unmuzzled.

The complainant, a lad, said on Sunday week he was passing Shepherd's-bush common when a dog ran from underneath one of the seats and bit his leg. He had a mark on his leg, and four holes in his trousers. Mr. Paget inquired for the dog and was told by Mr. Read, who defended, that it was outside and the principal feature of his case. (The dog was brought into the court, and created some amusement by running on to the bench and jumping up to the magistrate in a playful manner. It then jumped on to one of the chairs, and remained sitting during the hearing of the case.) Mr. Paget said it appeared a quiet dog. Mr. Read stated that he could give it a good character as a quiet, peaceable dog.

Mrs. Gordon was seated on the green, the dog playing near her, when the complainant, with another lad, came along snapping their fingers and throwing their arms about, which gave the dog an invitation to join them in a little fun.

Mr. Paget said the dog was young and playful, but he did not think it was desirable that one of that kind should be romping about a place used for the recreation of children. It should be kept under proper control. After Mr. Read had called attention to the Act, Mr. Paget dismissed the summons, as he could not say it was a dangerous dog.

(27.09.1879)

## A FACETIOUS JEW

Baron Aaron, a Jew, and dealer in cheap jewellery, who gave his address as 70, Cleveland-street, Whitechapel-road, was charged at Guildhall with causing an obstruction on the footway in New Broad-street, by selling cheap jewellery.

Edwin Whiteway, 100, said that on Tuesday evening, about seven o'clock, the prisoner created an obstruction by selling cheap jewellery on the footway in New Broad-street, and foot passengers had to go into the road to get past him. He asked him to go away, but he refused, and he was obliged to take him into custody in order to remove the obstruction. The defendant was very abusive, and they had great trouble to get him to the station-house.

The defendant said that he was born in England, and wanted to earn an honest living, but the police would not let him. It would be better for the inhabitants of the city if they looked after the thieves, instead of looking after him. He produced a toy of a girl skipping by turning a wire, and said that that was one of his articles of trade. He then went on to say that the officer Whiteway and his companion fancied themselves Dick Whittington and their cats, but they had not their cats with them; so he took one and offered it to him (Whiteway). Here the defendant pulled a pretty little buff kitten out of a bag and placed it on the table before Mr. Roe, the chief officer of the court, amid much laughter.

The defendant went on to state that he also offered another to the other officer, so that there might be two Dick Whittingtons – (loud laughter) – but they would not receive them. He produced from his bag a second

39

A FACETIOUS JEW

kitten, the counterpart of the first, and put that on the table also, to the amusement of the whole court.

He then went on to state that he had arrived by train just before he was taken, and had been playing a mouth organ (he commenced playing the mouth organ in court amid roars of laughter), but the police would not let him alone. He produced from his pocket two speaking dolls, dressed as police constables, who raised their hands, with staves in them, whenever their stomachs were squeezed. Those things, he said, were of more use to the City than their brothers in blue (the police) – (laughter) – and it would be better if they look after pickpockets and let respectable people like him alone.

Yowall, the gaoler, said the defendant had been here twice for obstruction. On the first occasion he was discharged, but on the second he was sent to prison. Alderman McArthur told the defendant that he could not be allowed to obstruct the thoroughfares, and his remarks about the police were most improper. He had been sent to prison for seven days for a similar offence, and it seemed to have had no effect upon him; he must therefore pay a fine of 20s., or go to prison for fourteen days with hard labour.

(06.09.1879)

## AN ACROBAT IN TROUBLE

At Worship-street Police-court, Joseph Morris, twenty-six, described as an acrobat, living at a common lodging-house in Flower and Dean-street, Spitalfields, was charged with having stolen a hat, coat and vest, value 16s., the property of William Cyrus Silverwood.

AN ACROBAT IN TROUBLE

The prosecutor, a boiler maker, living in Church-row, Limehouse, said that on Thursday last the prisoner got into conversation with him in Bishopsgate-street. The prisoner had been doing the "rope-tying trick" in the street, and he, prosecutor, had helped to tie him up. Afterwards the prisoner treated him to some ale, and thus they got into conversation.

Later on, the prisoner induced him to allow himself to be tied up before a crowd of persons. When the prisoner had tied him up, he picked up the prosecutor's coat, hat, and waistcoat, which had been taken off while the rope was fastened, and ran off with them.

Somebody cut the rope and set the prosecutor free, but the prisoner had then disappeared. The prosecutor gave information at the police-station, and the prisoner was apprehended on Sunday by Police-constable 148 H. He altogether denied the charge. At the station, however, having been identified by the prosecutor, who found the prisoner then wearing his waistcoat, the prisoner said that the prosecutor had got his rope and that he (prisoner) had left his coat behind.

The prosecutor produced it, but it was a mass of rags, and the rope, he said, had to be cut to pieces to get it off him, from the manner in which the prisoner had tied him up. The constable said the prisoner was under police supervision, having been convicted, and Mr. Hannay thereupon committed him for trial.

(15.11.1879)

# PUSHING A BOY INTO THE WATER

At the Central Criminal Court, before Baron Huddleston, John McIntyre, twenty-one, and James Murphy, thirty-one, were charged, the former, with throwing an Indian lad, named Kakook Ali, into the Victoria Dock, with intent to murder him, and the latter with aiding and abetting in the commission of the offence. Mr. De Michele prosecuted on behalf of the Treasury; the prisoners were defended by Mr. Edward Thomas.

The prisoners were engaged as seamen on board a vessel called the "Denmark" which was lying at the Victoria Dock, and on the afternoon of Oct. 25 was about to sail on a voyage. The prisoners, it appears, with several other shipmates, had been larking and drinking on shore during the morning, and on returning to their vessel they met the prosecutor, a lad of twelve, who was engaged as a cabin-boy on board another vessel lying in the Victoria Dock. The boy was standing on a "dummy" between the "Denmark" and another vessel, and McIntyre, as he passed him, seized him by the arms and threw him into the water.

Mr. Angrove, a superintendent employed by the company, immediately seized McIntyre, but the moment he did so Murphy drew a knife and threatened to stick him if he did not let McIntyre go. A quartermaster in the service of the company, named Hayward, came up to Mr. Angrove's assistance, and Murphy threatened him also, and attempted to "butt" him with his head and was very violent. Both prisoners, however, were eventually secured, and McIntyre, who was, no doubt, very drunk, said he had no intention to hurt the boy, and merely threw him into the water for a joke.

Mr. Thomas, on behalf of the prisoners, urged that McIntyre had merely been guilty of a foolish drunken sot, which he now deeply regretted, and that he never had the slightest intention to drown the boy; and as to Murphy, it was argued that he knew nothing more than that his drunken shipmate had been prevented from going on board the vessel, and he interfered to protect him.

The jury, after deliberating for a short time, wished to know if they could find the prisoner guilty of an assault. Baron Huddleston told them that they could not do so on the indictment now before them; but there was another indictment charging them with assault. The jury upon this returned a verdict of not guilty. They were then charged upon another indictment with assaulting Mr. Hayward, with intent to prevent their lawful apprehension. They pleaded guilty to this charge, and Baron Huddleston sentenced McIntyre to twelve months' imprisonment with hard labour, and Murphy to six months with hard labour.

(06.12.1879)

PUSHING A BOY IN THE WATER

# ZULUS IN COURT

At the Westminster Police-court last week, the manager to Mr. Farini, at the Royal Aquarium, attended with five newly imported Zulus. They were of various colours, but they all came from Natal. They attracted considerable notice in the streets and in the court by their manner and peculiar dress, all wearing boots, one corduroy trousers, and another having a pair of military overalls; three of them wore earrings, and to their large Italian-shaped hats gaily-coloured ribbons were suspended.

They placed themselves in front of the dock. They were, with one exception, men of fine stature and bearing apparently not more than twenty-one years of age. The smallest of the group called himself "Squash," and he was asked to act as interpreter, but when Mr. Webb, the

ZULUS IN THE WESTMINSTER POLICE COURT.

chief usher, handed him the New Testament, and asked him if he were a Christian, he merely replied "No Manilla," and in consequence was not sworn but merely informed the court of what the others said.

Mr. Partridge was handed a document and read it slowly. It set forth that articles of agreement had been entered into between W.J.Culley and J.A.Farini, by which the latter agreed to take and pay five Zulus £3 per month, and provide them with board and lodging, always retaining one month's salary in hand, the said Zulus agreeing to perform, sing, dance, &c., to illustrate the habits of their country, where the said Farini should think fit; and never to go out in the street without the permission of the said Farini or those in whose charge they may be, the agreement to last six months from Dec.11, with power to continue it for three or six months longer on the same terms. The document was signed by Nomanquasane (Squash), Inconda (Jim), Maquasa (Sam), Inaquala (Charley), Istri (John) – the names in parentheses representing their nicknames in English – and the agreement was witnessed by Zazel, Robinson and Culley. Mr. Partridge inquired of Mr. Culley – who brought the men over – what complaint they had to make.

Mr. Culley said Squash only was satisfied with the bargain he had entered into, but the others would not do anything, Sam and Charley being exceptionally troublesome. They had been performing a month in Paris, and although they had been offered £5 a month they even refused that. Through the man Squash, Jim, who gesticulated violently, biting his lips and clenching

his fist, at first said that he wanted £6 per month, and then £6.10s.; and concluded by declaring that he had been fighting the white man, and would either go back and do it again, or serve Mr. Culley, with whom he engaged, and he knew only one master, Mr. Culley. Mr. Culley said he had done with the matter altogether.

In reply to the magistrate, through the interpreter, the men expressed themselves dissatisfied with the way in which they had been treated. Mr. Partridge suggested, as they seemed to prefer to act under the instructions of Mr. Culley, whether it would not be better for him to be with them for say fourteen days, and then, perhaps, they would understand better the terms of their engagement. The manager replied that this was not possible, for Mr. Culley lived in Africa, and was desirous of going home as soon as possible. Mr. Culley stated that they had cost him £300 already, and he would not have anything more to do with them for a single day or hour.

In Paris they got out into the street, took too much to drink, and smashed a very valuable mirror, for which he had to pay, but this was deducted from their wages. The manager urged that they had been offered £6 a month, but they wanted to go in the street and do as they liked. Mr. Partridge, referring to the agreement, said surely they had some liberty. The manager replied that they were taken out in carriages and allowed some exercise under proper control. He had had no trouble with the other Zulus who had been performing at the Aquarium.

The men again said they were owed money, whereupon the manager and Mr. Culley produced some to pay them, but in a few moments the Zulus stated that nothing was due. Mr. Partridge observed that all he could do was to advise them to act up to their agreement, which they seem to have understood and signed; if not they would be sued in the county court, and they would have to pay the damages. "Squash" then explained that they had better do as they were told, and they left the court," Jim" especially making peculiar noises.

Later in the day they returned with the manager, who wanted to lock them up for breach of contract; but he was told that this could not be done, and he left the court very dissatisfied. After the usual court hours – Mr. Partridge having sat longer than usual – four of the men came back, and "Charley" for the first time spoke good English, and complained that they had not been paid, and preferred to work for another master. Mr. Partridge, on this gave directions to find them food and lodgings for the night, and stated that Mr. Safford, the chief clerk, would write to Mr. Chesson, the secretary of the Aborigines Protection Society.

(27.12.1879)

# A BEAR IN A POLICE COURT

Bears of every denomination should be made to understand that they will be welcome to this country in a managerial capacity. We shall be delighted to see them at the Zoological Gardens, or they are at liberty to travel about in a state of confinement; but when it comes to emulating Terpischore in the public streets Bruin must be taught that, among a people of whom it is said that they take their pleasure sadly, few things are more difficult to obtain than a dancing licence.

A large and intelligent bear, accompanied by a couple of peasants from the Bas-Pyrenees, appeared in the dock at Worship-street Police-court the other day, charged with capering at Clapton. As the peasants were more innocent of English even than of soap and water, it was explained to the bear that, though he had waltzed through France and danced all the way from Dover, his was a form of exercise which was not publicly recognised in the metropolis.

The bear, a harmless and well-conducted person, who stood on his hind legs and bowed to the magistrate's decision, left the court satisfied that it is to the advantage of his species that we should confine our encouragement of dangerous performances to men, women, and children.

(22.05.1880)

# THE OATH QUESTION

When the question of Mr. Bradlaugh's admission to Parliament and the legality of his oath of allegiance is being discussed in committee, two amusing cases occurred last week which serve to show the wretched mockery of the oath in every form. One of these occurred in the Central Criminal Court.

Neptune Love, twenty, was indicted for assaulting a Chinaman. The oath administered to the complainant was in the form of presenting him with a saucer, which he was required to break. He made two ineffectual attempts to do this, and the third time threw it with such force that it broke into a number of pieces, which fell in a shower of fragments on the jury-box, and caused a good deal of laughter in the court. After the saucer had been broken, a Chinese interpreter addressed the witness and said, "The saucer is broken, and if you do not speak the truth you will be broken the same as the saucer."

A BEAR IN A POLICE COURT

THE OATH QUESTION AT THE CENTRAL CRIMINAL COURT. – CHINAMAN BREAKING THE SAUCER

The complainant stated that on the 21st of May, he was in the West-India-road, Poplar, when the prisoner and another man came up to him; the prisoner struck him and the other man took some money out of his pockets and ran away. It appeared that a bill charging the prisoner with robbery was sent before the grand jury, but they ignored it, and returned a bill for assault only. The defence was the transaction was merely of the nature of what is called "a lark" and the prosecutor gave the defendant great provocation. The jury returned a verdict of not guilty.

On the 29th ult., at the Thames Police-court, Eliza Meyer, twenty-two, was charged with stealing a gold watch-chain, the property of Charles Brown, steward on board ship. On the prosecutor, who is a big-built African, stepping into the witness-box, the oath was administered to him in the usual form by Mr. Odell, the chief usher, and the book presented to him to kiss. He, however, pushed it gently from him, and said, "Me no kiss dat book sar, tank you all de same."

Mr. Lushington: What do you say?

Prosecutor: I no want to kiss dat book, sar. I got my chain back; dat's all I want.

Mr. Lushington: You have given this girl into custody for robbing you, and I must hear what you have to say against her.

Prosecutor (with great gravity): Jes so, sir; but I radar not. What for me hurt de gal? She's a berry nice sort of a gal. Me no want to send her to chokey.

Mr. Lushington: What do you know of the case, constable?

Police-constable Westeman, 338 K, said that all he knew of the matter was that prosecutor came to the Piggott-street Station, Limehouse, and complained of the defendant having robbed him. Witness afterwards went and apprehended the prisoner, and took her to the station, where the female searcher found the chain upon her. When the charge was read over to her she said that the prosecutor had made her a present of the chain.

Mr. Lushington (to prisoner): The prosecutor refuses to give evidence against you, and you will therefore be discharged. (To the constable) Let the chain be given to the person in whose possession it was found.

The prosecutor left the court, looking very foolish at the decision of his worship.

(12.06.1880)

THE OATH QUESTION AT THE THAMES POLICE COURT – A FORGIVING DARKIE –

# THE CHARGE AGAINST A NURSE – EXTRAORDINARY SENTENCE.

At the Central Criminal Court, Louise Ingle, a nurse of Guy's Hospital, surrendered on Thursday, to take her trial for the manslaughter of one of the patients in that establishment by negligence in the performance of her duty. Mr. Poland opened the case at some length, and said that the charge against the prisoner was that she had, by her negligence, caused the death of a woman, twenty-five years of age, named Louisa Morgan.

The prisoner was a nurse at Guy's Hospital, and on the 9th of June deceased was admitted into that establishment as a consumptive patient, and she was placed under the immediate attention of Dr. Percy, one of the physicians, and until the 4th of July she appeared to be going on favourably, and on that day she was cheerful and appeared to be improving in health.

It appeared that, in consequence of something that occurred on the fifth of July, the prisoner was angry with the deceased, and with the knowledge of the sister of the ward, the prisoner placed the deceased in a bath for the purpose of cleansing her, and without taking care that the bath was of a proper warmth, she placed the deceased first in an empty bath, and left her there in that condition for nearly three-quarters of an hour, and the patient appeared to be shivering with cold.

The prisoner's attention was called to this state of things, and she replied that deceased would not assist herself through obstinacy. Eventually the deceased was assisted back to her bed, and on the same day a very great change was observed in the appearance of the deceased. She appeared to be very much worse, and the prisoner's attention was called to the fact. It appeared that a quantity of cold water had been placed in the bath while the deceased was in it, and the deceased complained of

having been kept for so long a period in the cold. After that she continued to get worse and worse and on the 21st of July she died.

On Sunday the 4th of July she was visited by her husband and she then appeared cheerful, and, as he described it, "getting on nicely." On the following Wednesday her husband saw her again, and she then appeared to have complained of the prisoner having placed her in the bath, and he noticed some bruises on the arms of the deceased. He called the attention of the prisoner to these bruises, and told her that if anything happened to his wife she would be called upon for an explanation.

The trial lasted two days, Judge Hawkins summing up on Friday. He recounted the circumstances under which the deceased was admitted to the hospital, and said that there could be no doubt that the eventual cause of her death was not consumption, as was at first supposed, but the inflammation of the brain, and he thought also there could be no doubt that this fatal disease existed at the time the deceased was first admitted to the hospital, and that it went on increasing until the time of her death. While in that condition, it appeared that the deceased was directed to be placed in a cleansing bath, and the prisoner was authorised to place her in this bath. This being the case it was alleged that the prisoner had violently and harshly forced the deceased into the bath, and kept her in it for an unreasonable time, and that this treatment had had the effect certainly of accelerating, if not actually causing the death of the deceased.

The jury having retired, returned into court at one o'clock, and found the prisoner guilty, and at the same time expressed their opinion that there was great negligence in the nursing in the institution, and more careful supervision should be shown in its management.

On Saturday the prisoner was brought up for judgement. Several witnesses were called, and spoke to her previous character, but Mr. Poland said he thought he ought to inform the Court that complaint had been made of the conduct of the defendant towards a patient in another institution where the prisoner had been employed as nurse.

Mr. Justice Hawkins, addressing the prisoner, said that after a long inquiry, the jury had found her guilty of the manslaughter of one of the patients. He was sorry to see the difference of feeling that existed among the authorities of the hospital, who ought to have no other desire than to co-operate cordially in relieving the misery of the poorer classes entrusted to their charge, but he should not allow this in any way to influence the sentence he was about to impose. There could be no doubt that by her misconduct she had accelerated the death of the deceased, at all events for a short period. He did not believe that she was actually aware of the condition of the deceased, but still she must have known that she was treating her most improperly, and there was no doubt that she had accelerated the death.

Under all circumstances the sentence he should pronounce was that she be imprisoned for three months, without hard labour; and he said he hoped that this sentence would be a sufficient warning to other persons in her position not to be guilty of a similar case.

(14.08.1880)

DUEL WITH TEA CUPS

## A DUEL WITH TEA CUPS

At Woolwich Police-court, Joseph Cope, a chimney-sweep, living at Eltham, was charged with unlawfully wounding his wife, who appeared with her face half hidden in bandages, and said that she did not want to punish him.

Being informed that she must state the circumstances of the case, she proceeded, with some hesitation, to say that on the previous evening, when her husband came home to tea, they had a little wrangle, as usual, about money matters, because he would always keep the cash and make her an insufficient daily allowance to maintain the family. He aggravated her to such an extent that she took up a teacup and threw it at him, but missed him, and thereupon he threw one at her, but that missed also. She then threw a second cup, which went over his head, but he took good aim the second time, for his cup struck her forehead, and inflicted a long, deep wound.

They had had many a quarrel before, but this was the first time she had locked him up, and she begged the magistrate not to send him to prison.

A police-sergeant said that when the prisoner was given into custody his wife accused him of striking her with the cup while he held it in his hand, and he did not deny it. The officer added that he had often to make peace between them, and that there were faults on both sides. Mr. Balguy bound the prisoner in £5 to keep the peace for six months.

(18.09.1880)

## A GIRL OF SIXTEEN CARRYING HER DEAD CHILD IN THE STREETS

Mr. Humphreys held an inquest on Thursday at Mile End, touching the death of the newly-born male child of Elizabeth Brewer, who was seen on Sunday carrying the body in a parcel about the streets, and was taken into custody by a police-constable.

Margaret Kelly, of 8, Victoria-road, Mile End, said that on Monday week she saw Brewer sitting on a doorstep crying, with some men around her. She had two parcels. This was at half-past eleven at night. She took her home and gave her a night's lodging, and Brewer put her parcels in a cupboard, but at night she put them under her head and slept on them.

Witness said she suspected she had been delivered of a child, and accused Brewer of having confined recently, but this was denied. On the following Thursday a nasty smell was noticed in the room; but Brewer would not let her go to the cupboard, as she said there was nothing there belonging to witness. On Friday night Brewer went out and remained out all night, and she did the same thing on Saturday night. On Sunday witness went to the cupboard and found one of the parcels to contain the body of a child. She then went to find Brewer, who in the meantime returned and took the parcels with her. She told a police-constable but he would not do anything. When Brewer got into the street a large crowd assembled round her, as it soon got to be known that she had the body of a baby in the parcel. Police-constable Nicholas said he saw the crowd in the Commercial-road on Sunday and took possession of the parcel which Brewer was carrying. He asked her what she had in it and she replied her child. He sent for a cab and took her to the police-station. The parcel was afterwards found to contain the dead body of a child...

The jury returned a verdict that the child was still-born. Brewer, who is very ill, and at the infirmary, will be charged at the police-court with concealment of birth.

(27.11.1880)

A·GIRL·OF·16·CARRYING·HER·DEAD·CHILD·ABOUT·THE·STREETS,

## RAID UPON A "CRIMPS" BOARDING HOUSE

On Saturday morning a remarkable scene occurred in Limehouse-causeway at a lodging and boarding house specially devoted to Chinese and other Asiatic seamen.

It appears that a week or two since the ss. "North," commanded and owned by a Mr. Samuel Peter, arrived in the Victoria Docks from Calcutta, a large proportion of her crew being composed of Chinese and Lascar seamen, who had signed articles for a voyage to England and thence back to Calcutta.

Very soon after the "North" had been berthed, a number of the Asiatic seamen on board went away, after receiving a considerable advance on their wages for the voyage, and although every effort was made to discover their whereabouts, for some days nothing could be seen or heard of them.

At last the "serang" or boatswain of the Asiatics, returned to the vessel, and, after expressing contrition for having gone away without leave, informed the captain that the rest of the crew were at the house of a well-known crimp and boarding master in Limehouse-causeway, who had enticed them away from their own vessel, in order, as he stated to them, to put them on board another ship going back to their native place, on which they would receive higher wages than they had signed for on the "North;" his real object, however, being to receive so much per head for the men from other captains who were on the look-out for Asiatics to work their ship.

In consequence of this information Captain Samuel Peter, acting on magisterial advice, applied to the police for assistance to enable him to recover his men and send them on to Glasgow, where, in the meantime, the ship had left for.

Therefore, Inspector Thomas Reid, with Sergeant Patrick Fitzgerald and a body of men of the K Division, went to the house of the boarding master in question at Limehouse-causeway, and asked to see the proprietor. On his making his appearance he was asked by Captain Peter whether he had any men there belonging to the "North." He at once promptly replied that he had not. Inspector Reid, however, accompanied the captain into a room in the house, where they discovered two of the missing men comfortably engaged in opium-smoking. These were at once secured and handed over to safe custody.

Other rooms were then entered but the alarm had spread, and the unwilling Asiatics had to be dragged from under beds and tables, cupboards, &c.- in fact from every spot which had seemed likely to afford a hiding-place. After some resistance the whole of them were secured and marched out of the house.

In the street, however, things had assumed a very threatening aspect. A crowd of Chinese, Malay, and Lascar seamen had collected. Loud murmurs arose from them, and it was feared a rescue would be attempted. The police, however, closed round their prisoners and conveyed them to the Strangers' Home in the West India Dock-road. Here they were detained for a short time, and then conveyed to the Broad-street Railway Station, placed in the train under guard and started on their way to Glasgow to rejoin their ship.

The man from whose house they were taken is a well-known crimp, and has been complained of numerous times for decoying Asiatic seamen away from the vessels in which they belong.

(07.05.1881)

## ATTEMPT TO THROW A BICYCLIST

At Brentford Petty Sessions, Henry Brown, a costermonger, was summoned for assaulting a young gentleman, named Frederick Giffford, by attempting to throw him from the bicycle he was riding. According to the prosecutor's statement, he was proceeding, with two friends, through Brentford on bicycles, in single file, about seven o'clock in the evening, when he saw prisoner and other men in the road.

He, being first, blew his whistle, and rang his bell, but prisoner and the men would not get out of the way, and witness had to go on the wrong side of the road to pass. In passing prisoner the latter ran from where he was standing, caught hold of his leg, and tried to throw him from his machine, and would have succeeded had he not held on very tight.

The chairman said it was fortunate for the prisoner that this was a first offence. Had the prosecutor fallen from the bicycle he might have been killed. Prosecutor said he should not have brought the case forward if the prisoner had apologised. The magistrates fined the defendant 20s.

(02.07.1881)

ATTEMPT TO THROW A BICYCLIST
AT BRENTFORD

# EXECUTION OF LAMSON

*Dr. Lamson was a morphine addict who failed to instil any confidence in his patients and was dogged with financial problems. He stood to inherit £1,500 upon the death of his brother-in-law who doted on him. The young man was probably poisoned when aconitine was administered to a slice of fruitcake.*

*There was some evidence that Lansom was slowly becoming a bit of a fruitcake himself. He would often fire a revolver out of his bedroom window, swearing that the Turks were assembling down the street in preparation for an attack upon the house.*

Lamson woke on Friday morning last week at an early hour, after having had a tolerably good night's rest. Soon after he rose the chaplain of the gaol entered the condemned cell, and from that moment forward, save during the interval of breakfast, the convict was engaged in devotional services.

On the previous day the scaffold had been got ready, and, consequently, there was no noise to disturb the culprit as he ate or pursued his devotions. The drop, used on two previous occasions, had already been fitted together, and that had been duly inspected by Marwood on the afternoon before. It is true that the executioner on arriving at the gaol had found the pit to be of an insufficient depth, and had directed that an additional eighteen inches should be dug out; but this had occasioned no noise, and for several hours prior to the execution Lamson heard nothing to distract his thoughts. The evening preceding had been spent revising his private business, writing letters to friends, arranging monetary affairs, and generally concluding whatever communications he desired to make with his relatives. Then came retirement and sleep.

About a quarter to nine o'clock the bell of the gaol began to toll, greatly disturbing the condemned man, who now learnt that his time had nearly come. Very shortly afterwards the Under-sheriff, the deputy-governor of the gaol, the surgeon, and four warders made their appearance in the cell, with a view to prepare the convict for his last act. At Wandsworth it seems they have a curious custom. Usually in other gaols it is the custom to pinion the prisoner inside his cell, a mode both convenient and commendable. But, for reasons best know to themselves, the officials of this prison prefer to have this operation performed in the open air.

Thus it happened that Lamson, who had donned the suit of black which he wore at his trial, was allowed to walk freely from his cell between two warders, at about five minutes to nine, in the direction of the scaffold. That structure chanced happily to be hidden from the point of view of the door by which the culprit emerged by a corner of the wall, so that he could not see either it or the grave newly dug at first.

On the procession went, formed in the following order:- Two warders bearing white wands; then the clergyman of the gaol, in surplice and hood; next the convict, supported by two warders, who at this period had no necessity to assist him in walking; and finally, the deputy-governor and the surgeon, with several more warders. Marwood, who just then was waiting within the inner gates, with his straps thrown over his arm, only hesitated till the cortege should come near him. As it happened Lamson had not seen him, and apparently had not expected him, when the leading warder came up to the place where the executioner was. Then there was a sudden pause, for Marwood, with uplifted hand, had called out "Halt!" and the procession had stopped. That word "halt" told its tale upon the prisoner. Realising to the full his position for the first time, to all seeming, Lamson now staggered and almost fell against one of the warders who supported him. His tremour was, indeed, terribly apparent, and it was a great question for a moment whether he would not fall.

But the executioner at this instant came to his aid, and with the help of the warders kept him in an upright position. Not removing the collar which Lamson had put on, and only turning in the points, which might presently stand in the way of the rope, Marwood began to pinion him.

"I hope you will not hurt me," the convict murmured, half in fear and half by way, possibly, of remonstrance.

"I'll do my best not to hurt you; I'll be as gentle as I can," responded Marwood, and the work went on. Marwood's plan here was apparent. Lamson was a more powerfully-built man than he appeared, weighing upwards of eleven stone twelve pounds, and the executioner, evidently thinking that his strength would operate somewhat against a sharp and quick fall, fastened back his shoulders in a manner which precluded all possibility of the culprit resisting the action of the drop.

At last the gallows was reached, and here the clergyman bade farewell to the prisoner, while Marwood began his preparations with the rope and the beam overhead. With a view to meet any secretion of fear which might now befall the culprit, a wise provision had been made. The drop was so arranged as to part in the middle, after the fashion of two folding doors; but lest the doomed man might not be able to stand upon the scaffold without assistance, two planks of deal had been placed over the drop, one on each side of the rope, so that up to the latest moment, the two warders supporting the convict might stand securely and hold him up, without danger to themselves or inconvenience to the machinery of the gallows.

In this way Lamson was now kept erect while Marwood fastened his legs and put the cap over his eyes. He must have fallen had the arrangement been otherwise, for his effort to appear composed had by this time failed. Indeed from what now occurred it is evident that the convict yet hoped for a few moments more of life, for as Marwood proceeded to pull the cap down over his face he pitifully begged that one more prayer may be recited by the chaplain. Willing as the executioner possibly might have been to listen to this request, he had of course no power to alter the progress of the service, and was obliged to disregard this last demand of the dying man.

Signalling to the warders to withdraw their arms, he drew the lever which released the bolt under the drop, and so launched the prisoner into eternity. The clergyman finished the Lord's Prayer, in the midst of which he found himself when the lever had been pulled, and then, pronouncing the benediction, moved slowly back to the prison.

Of course, the body hung in its place for an hour, in accordance with the law, after which it was taken down and placed in a shell coffin for the purpose of inspection.

During the afternoon Mr. G.H. Hull, one of the coroners for Surrey, held an inquest on the body of Lamson. Evidence as to identity having been produced, Dr. Wyntner, the surgeon of Wandsworth Prison, stated that he had examined the body of the deceased, and that death, which had been instantaneous and painless, was due to apoplexy.

It was on December 3rd last year that Lamson committed the murder for which he on Friday morning answered with his life in Wandsworth Gaol. His victim being his brother-in-law, Percy John, a cripple suffering from disease of the spine. The youth was in his nineteenth year, and at the date of the murder was a scholar at Blenheim House School, Wimbledon.

On the day mentioned Lamson, in the presence of Mr. Bedrook, the principle of the academy, administered in a capsule sufficient aconitine to produce death. Lamson after the murder left England, but on December 8th presented himself at Scotland yard to report his whereabouts and was then taken into custody and charged with the wilful murder of Percy John.

From the Wandsworth Police-court he was remitted to the Old Bailey on the capital charge, and, after a trial extending from the 8th to the 14th of March, was found guilty by the jury and sentenced to death by Mr. Justice Hawkins. The execution was fixed for April 4th but representations from the President of the United States that affidavits of importance bearing on the sanity of the condemned man were being sent from America induced the Home Secretary to grant a reprieve to April 19th. Similar reasons were urged for a still further respite, and Friday, April 28th, was ultimately fixed as the date of execution.

(06.05.1882)

FRACAS AT THE ST JAMES'S RESTAURANT

## FRACAS AT ST JAMES'S RESTAURANT

Mr. P. Perkins, No. 23, Grove-road, Brixton, was summoned before Mr. Newton, at Marlborough-street, for an assault on Walter Wormington, and of the waiters at the St. James's Hall Restaurant, Regent-circus. There was a counter-charge of assault by Wormington on Mr. Perkins.

Mr. Roberts, Moorgate-street, appeared for Wormington, and stated that the assault arose out of the circumstances of the defendant having refused to pay one of the items on the dinner bill furnished to him and his party. It was one of the regulations of the restaurant that no customer was to give away any portion of a dish ordered by him to any friend that might be dining with him. If this were done two portions were to be paid for.

Mr. Newton thought this was a very unusual arrangement.

Mr. Roberts said it was stated on the bill of fare.

Mr. Newton said that was not binding.

The complainant Wormington was called, and he stated that the two cutlets having been ordered, which were partaken of by three of the company; three cutlets were charged in the bill, and on the defendant refusing to pay for more than two, he went and spoke to the proprietor, Mr. Grieve.

Mr. Newton: And what did Mr. Grieve say?

Witness: He told me to take his hat, and I did take it.

Mr. Newton: I think the public should be made aware of what they have to expect if they dine at the St. James's Restaurant. Is Mr. Grieve here?

Mr. Roberts: No, he is not; but I will send for him.

Mr. Newton: I think he ought to be here to hear what I have to say, for the sooner he is acquainted with the law the better.

Mr Grieve came into court, but the other business occupied the attention of the Court until the hour for closing, and it was arranged that the further proceedings should be adjourned for a week.

On the parties again appearing in court, Mr. Newton asked if Mr. Grieve was present.

Mr Roberts said he was not, but he would remind the magistrate he was in court for an hour last week waiting to be heard.

Mr. Newton: I think he should be here. I think it highly improper he is not here to hear what I shall think it right to say.

The case was then called on, Mr. Roberts appearing for the waiter, and Mr. Edward Lewis for Mr. Perkins.

Evidence was then given at some length in support of the charge and counter-charge; it appearing that the waiter had taken the hat of the defendant Mr Perkins, who had resisted the charge for the third portion of cutlet.

Mr. Newton said; I will first tell the keepers of taverns and restaurants through you (the waiters) that they have no lieu on the personal property of the guests. It was wrong to take the hat as stated, and the owner, in attempting to regain possession, was justified in committing any necessary act of violence to attain his object. With respect to the evidence I state at once I place no reliance whatever on what the waiters have said, and put the fullest reliance on what has been stated by Mr. Perkins. I am thoroughly shocked that such an occurrence should have been possible in England. Three gentlemen and two ladies go into a first-class restaurant for refreshment; one has his hat taken from him because an imposition is resisted; he is then attacked by the waiters, given into custody in the street, and taken to the station; and I am very sorry Mr. Grieve is not here to-day to hear me state what I think of the proceeding. The defendant will pay 60s. fine and 40s. expenses; and I dismiss the summons against Mr. Perkins.

(26.07.1882)

# THE HYDE PARK MYSTERY

The Hyde Park mystery, as it has been termed, is cleared up. It is quite certain that the ill-fated young woman met her death not by foul play but by an accident. Her face and body presented a most shocking appearance. Our artist has made an accurate sketch which will be found engraved on the top of the page in this week's number of the POLICE NEWS.

Mr. S.F.Langham held an inquiry at St. George's Hospital, Knightsbridge, on Monday, into the death of Mary Ann Message, whose body was recently found near Hyde Park. Mrs. Message, mother of the deceased, and the wife of a labourer of Pevensey, near Eastbourne, said her daughter, as far as she knew, was a single woman. Her age was twenty-four, and she had not seen or heard of her for over two years until now. When she came to London witness placed her under the care of a Mrs. Williams, but she did not know where she lived. It was through the Vicar of Pevensey that she went to Mrs. Williams

Martha St. John, of 34, Exeter-street, Sloane-street, a widow, deposed that the deceased, whom she knew as Annie Message, had resided with her for four weeks. She represented herself to witness as a dressmaker, but she did not believe that. She saw her alive on Monday night, she then being in her room with another girl who lived with her, She went out on Monday night and did not return. From what witness saw in the papers on Friday night she came to this hospital, and identified her body.

Jeannette Burnett, of the same address as last witness, said she saw the deceased at Knightsbridge on the Monday night she was so drunk she could scarcely walk. Witness was not sober either.

Dr. Lesley College, house surgeon, described the deceased's injuries, and said his impression was that a heavy wagon had gone over her.

David Grainger, of Castle-street, Leicester-square, a "Negro minstrel," said that between one and two o'clock on the morning of the 24th ult. he saw the deceased standing on the edge of the kerb near St. George's Hospital with a gentleman. The gentleman called out to witness "Sambo, I want you," but before he could get to them they both fell into the road. A heavy wagon laden with vegetables, going to Covent-garden, came by at the time, and witness tried to pull the deceased away; but it was too late, and the vehicle pushed over her. She was picked up and taken to the hospital. He was sure it was not possible for the gentleman to have avoided what happened. He believed the driver was not even conscious of what had happened as he did not stop. Another "minstrel" gave similar evidence.

Sergeant Grant said he had made inquiries of the whole of the wagoners who went past that night, and not one of them knew anything of it. The coroner having summed up, the jury returned a verdict of accidental death.

(11.11.1882)

## A LIVELY SCENE AT A SCHOOL

At one of the Metropolitan Police-courts, a young gentleman, who said that he was the head teacher situated within the district of the court, applied to the magistrate for a summons against a woman for assaulting him.

Applicant stated that for some time he and his scholars had been much annoyed by a boy – not belonging to the school – who was continually throwing stones at the windows or making a noise outside whilst the lessons were in progress; he was also in the habit of taking off the younger boys' caps and throwing them about.

On Thursday he began to throw stones at the windows, and applicant sent three of the elder boys to fetch him into the school, and at the same time dispatched a fourth for a policeman. The three scholars caught the boy, and carried him into the school, but whilst they were waiting for the arrival of the policeman, the boy's mother, who had been told by some person what had happened, rushed into the school, and seizing upon applicant commenced to assault him.

He struggled with her, but she, being a big powerful woman, managed to get him down upon the floor, and she then proceeded to belabour him with a stick which she had brought with her. After she had struck him a number of times she got up and went away, taking her boy with her.

The affair caused great confusion in the school, upsetting all the pupils and spoiling the morning's work completely. His worship said that under the circumstances he must decline to grant a summons, as it seemed to him that the applicant had been to blame in making a prisoner of the boy, as he said he had done.

(19.05.1883)

## SAVAGE ATTACK UPON A POLICEMAN

John Harris, Jane Reynolds and Alfred Lindsey were charged on remand, on Thursday last week, before Mr. Saunders, with being concerned with others not in custody, in committing a murderous assault on Dennis Mortimer, a constable of the K Division, who was lying in a serious condition at home. The prisoners were charged on Monday, but there was no witness present who witnessed the affair, the magistrate, after hearing the testimony of Herbert Brin, 436 K, adjourned the case until Tuesday.

Harris Marks, of 149 Upper North-street, Poplar, said that at half-past three o'clock on Sunday afternoon he heard loud cries of "Stop him," and he saw several lads run across a bridge, a short distance from his shop, followed by Constable Dennis Mortimer. He captured the prisoner Harris, and as he was bringing him back across

A LIVELY SCENE AT A SCHOOL

the bridge a mob of young ruffians infesting the district collected round him, and commenced pelting him with stones, and striking him with sticks they were carrying. The constable called to witness to protect him from the crowd in the rear, and tried to get Harris into two or three doorways to avoid the violence of the mob, but they closed the door in his face, and he was obliged to do the best he could against such odds.

As they turned an angle leading into Stainsby-road, Poplar, witness saw Harris and Mortimer struggling together in a desperate manner, and the crowd beating the constable about the body and head with sticks and hurling stones at him. Mortimer made strenuous efforts to retain Harris in custody, but he was rescued three times, and on drawing his staff to protect himself, the female Reynolds wrenched it from his hand, owing to his exhausted condition, and struck him on the side of the head with it, and another girl not identified by the witness also hit him about the head with the staff.

The prisoners and their gang effected their escape, leaving the constable insensible, and Marks took him into the passage of a house, got a glass of water for him, and with the aid of another man they supported him to the station. In answer to Mr. Saunders, Marks said the constable had his helmet on at the time the female struck him on the head with the staff, or the consequences might have been more serious. Mr. Saunders remanded the prisoners for a week for the injured man's attendance.

(02.06.1883)

## A WOMAN SHOT AT EPSOM ON THE DERBY DAY

On Thursday, at the Epsom Petty Sessions, before Mr. Trotter and other magistrates, John Talbot Ashenhurst, described as a coach painter, of the Surrey Yeoman public-house, Dorking, was charged with causing grievous bodily harm to Elizabeth Borer, the wife of a warehouseman, residing at Caterham Valley, near Croydon, on the racecourse on Derby Day.

Police-constable Patrick Storer, 22 R Reserve, deposed that at half-past five on the previous afternoon he was on duty at Epsom Downs, and received information that a woman had been shot. The prisoner was pointed out to him as the party who had fired the revolver. Witness went up to him and saw the revolver (produced) in his right-hand pocket, and having taken it out he conducted the prisoner to where the injured woman lay. He saw some blood on the ground, and Police-sergeant 42 E came and took charge of the woman, while witness took the prisoner to the station.

Witness told him he would be charged with causing grievous bodily harm to the woman, and he said it was accidental. He afterwards said he was firing at some bottles near a rifle gallery and that he had brought the revolver with him for that purpose. It was close to a rifle gallery where it occurred. There were five cartridge-cases in the revolver, and they had all recently been discharged by the prisoner. When he first took him into custody he was near a drinking-booth, and appeared to be getting some brandy for the woman.

SAVAGE ATTACK ON A POLICEMAN.

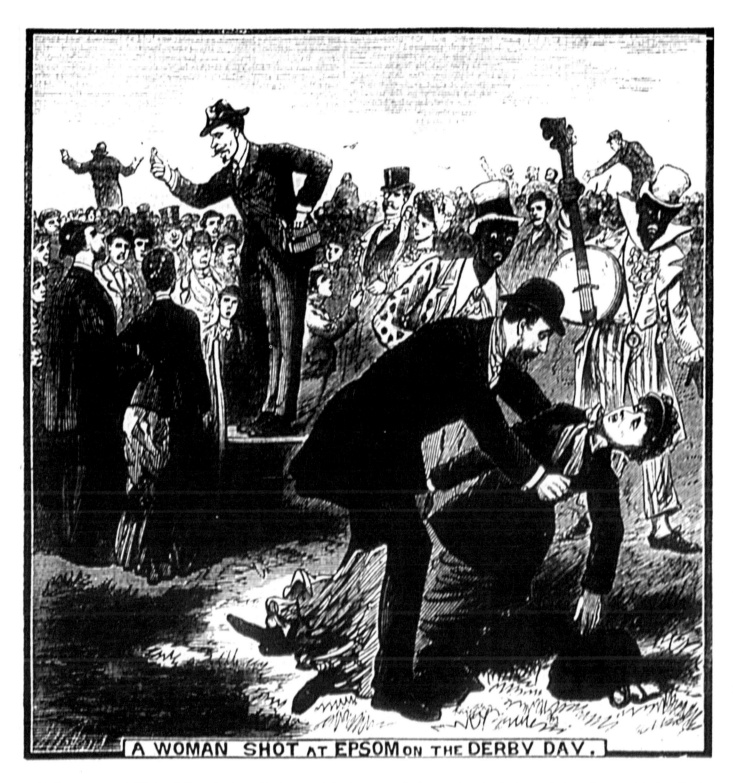

A WOMAN SHOT AT EPSOM ON THE DERBY DAY.

Police-sergeant Michael Crawford, 42 E, deposed that he was attracted to the spot by a crowd. He found the woman had been shot in the thigh. Pointing to the prisoner, the woman said, "That is the man who shot me, for why I don't know. I never saw him before."

The Chairman: Did she say he deliberately shot her?

Witness: No; she said "I felt I was shot and saw the revolver in his hand smoking."

With the assistance of some females, witness tried to stop the bleeding with some handkerchiefs, and afterwards conveyed her to the Epsom Infirmary, where she was seen by Dr. Coltait, who, after a consultation with the police-surgeon, said the woman had received a very dangerous wound in the left thigh, near the femoral artery. He added it was a case which should be taken to hospital forthwith.

Witness then hired two horses, and with the Union ambulance he took her during the night to Guy's Hospital, arriving there at four o'clock that morning. She was at once admitted. Witness saw Dr. Stokes, the house-surgeon, and he said the woman was in great danger and the limb would very likely be operated upon in the course of the day. The bullet had not been extracted. At the next hearing evidence would be adduced to show that the prisoner fired wantonly in the crowd, and the friends of the injured woman would tell the Bench that he fired at the gallery or bottles from the crowd. By the Magistrate: Prisoner appeared perfectly sober, but very strange. The prisoner was remanded. It was ascertained that he had eighteen ball-cartridges in his possession when taken into custody.

(02.06.1883)

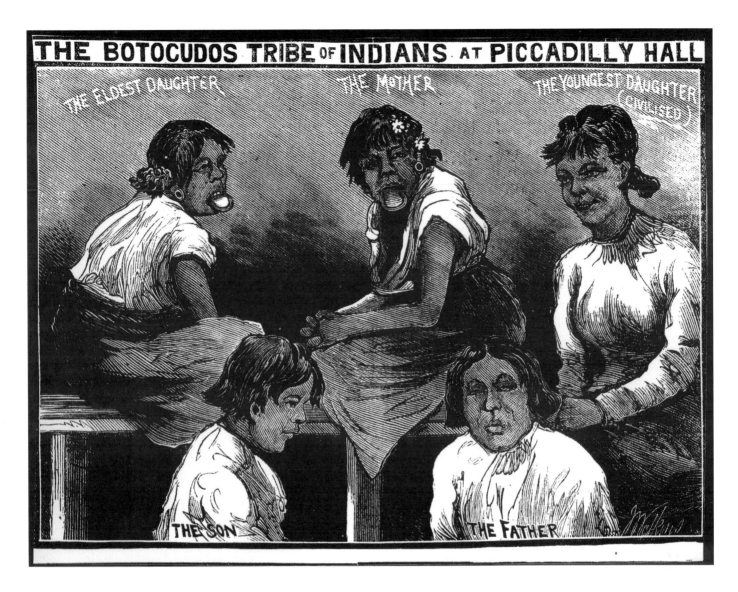

THE BOTOCUDOS TRIBE OF INDIANS AT PICCADILLY HALL

THE ELDEST DAUGHTER · THE MOTHER · THE YOUNGEST DAUGHTER (CIVILISED)

THE SON · THE FATHER

## THE ANTHROPOLOGICAL EXHIBITION AT THE PICCADILLY HALL

The reader will find on the top of the front page of this week's edition of POLICE NEWS portraits of the Botocudos tribe of Indians now being exhibited at Piccadilly Hall, together with engravings, utensils, and other interesting articles which form not the least interesting portion of the exhibition. At the cost of a heavy pecuniary outlay, and great personal exertions, attended by serious risk of life, have these rare and unique specimens of savage life been collected.

(09.06.1883)

## TERRIBLE MURDER AT WOOLWICH

At the Woolwich Police-court on Friday, William Hughes, 34, a coal porter, was charged with the wilful murder of his mother by beating her upon the head with a hammer at Union-gardens, Woolwich. The evidence previously given showed that the prisoner was a single man, and lived with his parents, both of whom are now dead.

On April 25 he went home rather late, and partly intoxicated. He was angry with his mother on the subject of his supper, and in a fit of temper made an attack upon her which he afterwards acknowledged in the presence of several witnesses, giving the hammer up to the policeman with the remarks, "That's what I did it with; smell it."

There was no one living in the house except the prisoner and his parents, and there are now no actual witnesses of the crime in existence, but the evidence, irrespective of the prisoner's admissions, was almost conclusive as to his guilt. The case was now conducted by Mr. Batchelor, on behalf of the Public Prosecutor.

Police-constable Tavner said that when he went to the house the prisoner said, "I suppose it will be murder. I hope she will die, and the old man too, for they are no good and ought to have been dead long ago. You had better let me finish her, and not let her lie there in misery."

George Rice, M.B., medical superintendent of the Woolwich Union Infirmary, at Plumstead, said that the deceased woman was admitted to the establishment at one o'clock suffering from numerous wounds on the head, from the effects of which she died on Saturday week…Those injuries had probably been caused by some blunt instrument such as the hammer produced, used with considerable violence. It was hardly possible that they could have resulted from falls, as the deceased woman herself asserted on her death-bed. She and her husband were both conscious when they made their depositions in the presence of the magistrate.

The prisoner in his defence said that he had no recollection of using the hammer, and must have been

TERRIBLE MURDER AT WOOLWICH

mad when he spoke to the policeman. He recollected pushing the old lady, who fell against the latch of the door, and then reeled into the washhouse and fell down. He had been drunk for a month right off.

Thomas Wisdom, a witness for the prisoner, said that he knew the prisoner had been drinking for several weeks, but doing his work as usual. When sober he was a very quiet man, but when drunk, he was like a madman. Mr. Marsham then committed the prisoner for trial for wilful murder.

(16.06.1883)

*Hughes was sentenced to five years for the lesser charge of manslaughter.*

## HORRIBLE MURDER OF A CHILD BY ITS FATHER

At Croydon on Monday, James Cole, described as a labourer, of 12, Pridham-road, New Thornton-heath, was charged with murdering his son Thomas, aged three years, by striking his head on the floor.

The prisoner, who is a short, spare man, of about thirty-five years of age, presented rather a dazed appearance on being placed in the dock, and when

Dr.Carpenter read the charge over to him and asked him the usual question as to whether it was true, he replied, "I decline to say anything to-day until I have seen my legal adviser."

Mrs. Cole, the wife of the accused, was about to get into the witness-box in a half-fainting condition, when Mr. Scale, the magistrate's clerk, pointed out that the woman could not be examined as a witness against her husband, such testimony being bad in law. The prisoner, with considerable bravado, then asked that all the witnesses should be ordered out of court, and the magistrate at once agreed to the application.

The first witness called by Chief-inspector Mason, (who conducted the prosecution) was Robert Gilbert, a painter living in Pridham-road. He deposed that the prisoner was a stranger to him. At half-past ten on Sunday night he was passing Cole's cottage, when he heard a woman's voice screaming "Murder!" He ran into the house, where in a front room he observed the prisoner holding a child up by its legs and swinging its head against the wall. He saw the head strike against the wall with great force.

The accused was about to swing the child round again, when witness seized him by the collar and pulled him out of the house. Cole then dropped the child, and witness had a desperate struggle with him, during which he (Gilbert) was obliged to strike him several blows. Ultimately releasing himself, Cole ran up the road, followed by witness, who again caught him and dealt him several more blows. When the prisoner dropped the child on the floor the mother picked it up.

The prisoner: Did you enter the house?

Witness: Certainly I did.

The prisoner: Speak the truth; now, be careful. Just think of my position.

Richard Cole, a boy of fourteen, who said he could not read, but knew the obligation of an oath, stated that he was a son of the prisoner. On Sunday night he was standing at the front garden gate waiting to go indoors, when his mother screamed, "Murder!" His father afterwards opened the door, and witness saw that he was holding his little brother Thomas up by the heels and that he bashed his head on the floor. While standing outside witness had heard two heavy thumps on the floor. The witness Gilbert had in the meantime arrived, and his father kept exclaiming, "Keep that man back."

Dr. Carpenter: Where was your mother all this time?

Witness: She had gone into a next-door neighbours, because father had been abusing her. I was afraid to go indoors because I thought father would knock me about. I have three brothers and sisters, and my mother put them to bed at nine o'clock. My father had not been beating any of the other children besides deceased.

Dr. Carpenter: What time did your father come home?

Witness: He had not been out during the day, but had been reading the newspaper all the evening. He had had neither beer nor spirits. He drank a little water. All the other children were asleep when this occurred.

In reply to a question put by the clerk, the witness Gilbert said no sound came from the child whilst it was being swung about.

The prisoner inquired whether he could have some one speak for him. He wanted counsel's advice, but had no money to pay for it. Dr. Carpenter said he would communicate with Chief-inspector Mason, and endeavour to get him what he desired. The prisoner was then remanded.

Prisoner, on being removed, was followed by a large crowd of persons who hooted and hissed him. One woman shouted that prisoner was a murderer, and should be hanged. "Hang him! Hang him!" she cried. "He ought to be lynched. Hand him over to the women and we'll limb him." Cole, who turned very pale, and cast a terrified look behind him, was, however, taken safely to the station.

On being put in the cell Cole put on a vacant stare, and inquired whether his child (the deceased) was alive. He was informed that it was dead, whereupon he burst into tears, and wept for some time. He also declared that a state of semi-starvation was the cause of his crime.

## CORONER'S INQUEST AND VERDICT

On Thursday Mr. W.P. Morrison held an inquiry at the Wilton Arms, Gillett-road, New Thornton-heath, as to the death of Thomas Cole, aged three years and eight months, who was murdered by his father, James Cole, at 11, Pridham-road West, on Sunday evening.

Richard Cole, a brother of the deceased, said his father was a brickmaker and labourer. Witness returned home at six o'clock on Sunday evening. His father had a meal after witness got home. His mother was sitting with him in the front room. There was quarrelling, and his father sticking a chisel into the middle of the floor said, "I will take your life before the night's out." There was only some bread in the house, and his father said he would take her life for keeping him without better food. His mother went to the gate, but later on suddenly ran back, and witness saw his father holding the deceased up by his feet and knocking his head on the floor. He then threw the child over his shoulder, and dropped him on the floor. The child had been lying on the bed. He believed his father injured the deceased because his mother was so fond of him. His father had only been out of prison three weeks, and had done no work since Christmas. He had said that he did not intend to work. His mother had been supporting her husband and family by mending chairs.

Robert Gilbert, of 1, Pridham-road West, deposed to seizing prisoner immediately after the murder.

Harriet Harding, a married woman, of 11, Pridham-road West, said on Sunday night she was talking to Mrs. Cole at the gate. As the woman was about to enter her house, she said, "Here goes, life or death!" and when she got to the door she clasped her hands and exclaimed, "Good God! What do you think? This villain of mine has got my dear baby by the heels as if he means to dash its brains out!"

With that she rushed in, and returned to the door crying, and saying, "Good God, he has murdered my baby!" The witness Gilbert then came up and collared Cole, and the mother picked up the baby, which had been lying on the floor, near the door, bleeding. Witness snatched the child out of its mother's arms, and sprinkled its face with water, and it gave one sigh. The child expired at twenty minutes past seven on Monday morning.

By the coroner: Cole was a very desperate man. His wife once jumped out of window while he was chasing her with a knife.

Dr. Mark Jackson, M.D., of Parchmore-road, said he was called to see the deceased between ten and eleven o'clock on Sunday night. There were marks of violence about the head and face. Injury to the brain was the cause of death. The injury would require great violence, and was probably caused by the head coming into violent contact with a plain, hard substance, like a floor or wall.

Inspector Robert Butlers, W Division, said about twelve o'clock on Sunday night he went to the house and saw Mrs. Cole, who said her husband told her to take his boots and get something to eat and some tobacco and beer, adding that if she did not he would murder some of the children. Witness examined the front room, and saw an old mattress lying on the floor, and at the foot of it one of Cole's boots, with a small quantity of blood close to it. There were a dozen bricks in one corner of the room. Cole had been sitting on them reading the newspaper. In an upstairs room there was another old mattress. The house was very dirty, and there was not a particle of furniture in the place.

The jury returned a verdict of wilful murder against James Cole, who was committed for trial.

(01.09.1883)

*Cole's defence was one of temporary insanity but he was found guilty and sentenced to death.*

HORRIBLE MURDER AT THORNTON HEATH-CROYDON.

## PRACTICAL JOKING AT THE COGERS HALL

In the Lord Mayor's Court, on Thursday, before the Assistant-Judge and a common jury, an action was brought by Mr. Edward Dring against Mr. Percy Judd, the part proprietor with Mr. Joseph Simmons of the Cogers Hall public-house, Little Bridge-lane, to recover compensation in damages for an assault he alleged the defendant had committed upon him, and also for the value of his clothes, which were damaged at the time – Mr. Sims was counsel for the plaintiff: Mr. Wildey Wright for the defendant.

The plaintiff said that on October 27 last year he went into the defendant's house with a friend named Green at about eight o'clock in the evening, and was looking through the door which leads from the bar to the billiard-

PRACTICAL JOKING AT THE COGER'S HALL.

room, when the defendant, who was fond of practical jokes, threw a bag of flour at him. It struck him on the hat and fell all over his clothes, causing jeers to be bandied about, such as "Old Father Christmas," "Old Boozer," &c (Laughter.)

On turning round to see where it came from he was met with a second bag of flour, and a dirty swab, full in the face, delivered by the defendant from behind his bar, he having taken the trouble to stand on a settle to do so, immediately after ducking under the table and running out into the street. The plaintiff followed him out, when a third bagful was thrown at him, catching his friend and placing him in a similar plight. That gentleman, on returning to the house, was attended to and brushed

down by the billiard marker; but he was a laughing-stock for all. (Laughter.)

He was over sixty years of age, and did not like a joke being played upon him. He therefore instructed his solicitors to claim £5 for the damage done, and an apology; but the defendant refused to take any notice of their letter, and the present action was brought.

Mr Sims: And now he pleads that he was not present at the time. The advice Old Weller gave to his son was "Try an alibi, Sammy." (Loud laughter.)

The defendant, his partner, and several witnesses were called, who swore that he, (the defendant) was not in the house at the time of the throwing of the swabs and flour. One of the witnesses said that all the flour that was actually thrown was thrown by himself. When the plaintiff came into the house, someone said, "Here comes old born drunk." (Roars of laughter.) Almost immediately someone took his hat off his head, and after putting a lot of flour in it, replaced it on his head. The old gentleman at once pulled it off, and the flour fell all over his clothes – in fact, he was smothered with it from head to foot. Witness's clothes were covered with it also, and he took up a handful and threw it at the old man – (laughter) – who rushed out into the street amidst a shower of swabs, and returned with a large stone, saying if he knew who it was that had played the joke on him he would "put it through his eye." (Renewed laughter). The stone was taken away from him, and ultimately he departed.

Mr. W. Wright: How did he look when he discovered the flour – savage?

Witness: I can't say. He looked remarkably white. (Loud laughter.)

Mr. W. Wright: Perhaps that was the outward and visible sign of an inward spiritual belief. (Roars of laughter.)

Witness: That I know nothing about.

The learned Assistant-Judge, in summing up, said the question for the jury to decide was whether the evidence supported the plaintiff's case that the defendant committed the assault; if so he was entitled to substantial damages. If they believed the defendant's witnesses he could not have committed it.

The jury found a verdict for the defendant.

(02.02.1884)

FATAL STRUGGLE AT MILLBANK.

# FATAL STRUGGLE AT MILLBANK

On Friday, Mr. A. Braxton Ricks, the deputy-coroner for Westminster, opened an inquiry in the library of Millbank Penitentiary into the circumstances attending the death of Agnes Jane Mayne, aged fifty-five years, chief matron of the prison, who died on Tuesday. Colonel Garcia, deputy-governor of the convict section of Millbank Prison, said the deceased had been in the service thirty years, and was in charge of the female convicts.

On the day of her death she had a prisoner named Elizabeth Johnson under her charge. That person was now in court. She was under a sentence of penal servitude for five years having been convicted at the Middlesex Sessions on April 7th of this year, and was received at Millbank on the 25th of the same month. Since her reception she had never been punished, nor had she ever been reported.

On Tuesday the deceased reported Johnson to witness for quarrelling and assaulting another convict, and witness proceeded with the deceased to the prisoner's cell. Upon arriving there witness found the prisoner locked in her cell, the outer door being open. Johnson stood up behind the bars, there being present the matron of the infirmary and Mr. Alexander of the Colonial Police, who was qualifying for the Prison Department.

The prisoner was excited, and threatened the other convict. Witness told her to be quiet till he had heard the charge, and she became quiet. With that, witness took the evidence of Matron Kerry, and in the result he awarded the prisoner bread and water for one day. She said she did not mind the punishment as she could not eat her food and therefore would not miss it. Witness and Mr. Alexander then withdrew, being followed by the deceased.

Hearing the prisoner scream, he turned round and saw another matron open her cell door, immediately afterwards Johnson rushed to the railings of the corridor, which were thirty feet from the ground, and had actually mounted them, apparently with a view to jumping over, when Matron Kerry seized her, and witness, the deceased and Mr. Alexander rushed to her assistance, prisoner meanwhile struggling very violently. Had it not been for Mr. Alexander, who behaved very manfully, the prisoner must have fallen on to the stone flooring below. The prisoner was replaced in her cell, still struggling and shrieking most violently, and witness signalled for a warder to bring handcuffs to restrain her.

As he did so he heard someone say, "Miss Mayne has fallen." Matrons Kerry and Packer and Mr. Alexander were in the cell with the prisoner, and the deceased was lying on the floor, by the door. Witness raised her, and she gave a sigh, and Mr. Alexander threw some water in her face. The prisoner was still struggling violently in a corner of the cell.

At this time Chief Matron Bragg arrived, and the deceased was removed to a ward and placed on a mattress. Dr. Carpenter then came upon the scene, and pronounced life extinct in Miss Mayne. The prisoner continued to struggle until the handcuffs were placed upon her. When she heard that Miss Mayne was dead she said, "I would not hurt Miss Mayne." Her object in struggling was evidently to precipitate herself over the railings. Colonel Garcia added that the deceased was actively engaged with the prisoner for about two minutes. It was voluntary on her part; it was not her duty except for humanity's sake.

The further evidence was corroborative of the above statements, and the medical testimony was to the effect that death was caused by syncope, aggravated or hastened on by excitement. The inquiry was adjourned.

(16 04.1884)

# A JEALOUS WIFE AND DISAPPOINTED BRIDE

At the Westminster Police-court Isabella Todd, thirty, well dressed, described as married, and residing at 2, Union-terrace, Kentish-town, was charged before Mr. d'Eyncourt with assaulting Miss Marian Jenner, a young lady, residing at Faversham. Some excitement was occasioned in court by the prisoner giving the complainant a violent smack in the face while the latter was making her way to the witness-box.

Complainant, who was smartly dressed, deposed that she was in London on a visit to her sister, who resided at 40, Aclam-road, Westbourne-park. She was with her sister on Saturday afternoon at Victoria Station waiting on the departure platform for a train to Faversham, when the prisoner came up in an excited manner, and gave her two blows over the head with an umbrella. The umbrella was broken by the force of the second blow.

When taken outside the station prisoner called her bad names and struck her twice in the face with her hand. Complainant's sister gave corroborative evidence, and Kitch, 543 B, deposed that he witnessed the assault in the street. On the way to the station prisoner was very excited, and stated that the complainant was living with her husband. The defendant said this was her defence.

Complainant, recalled, said she knew the prisoner as a resident of Faversham. Prisoner had lived with a man named Joseph Edward Hayes, and witness was engaged to be married to him. The banns were published at All Saints', Kensington, and the marriage was arranged for 24th March last, but the bridegroom did not appear. She had not seen him since, although her sister had heard from him. Prisoner said the man spoken of was her own husband, wedded to her in St. Martin's-in-the-Fields.

Mr. d'Eyncourt remarked that she had committed an apparently unprovoked assault, and unless she could find responsible bail he must remand her in custody. He advised her to communicate with her friends. Prisoner said she would do so, and produce her "marriage lines." In default of finding bail she was removed to the House of Detention.

(07.06.1884)

# THEFT BY A DOG AT BARKING

On Tuesday last week at Stratford Petty Sessions, William Wood, twenty-nine. A labourer of Padnell's-place, Axe-street. Barking, was charged with stealing on the 29th ult., half a pig's head, valued at 2s, the property

A JEALOUS WIFE AND DISAPPOINTED BRIDE.

THEFT BY A DOG AT BARKING.

of Thomas Brewer, a dairyman, of Park Dairy, Axe-street, Barking.

The evidence showed that at about a quarter to nine o'clock on Monday night, Mrs. Brewer, the wife of the prosecutor, was sitting in a room adjoining the shop, when she noticed a large dog in the place, and immediately afterwards heard the prisoner, who was outside, call out, "Fetch it here." Mrs. Brewer went to see what the dog had, when she saw him carrying half a pig's head and trotting by the side of the prisoner, who was going up the street. The prisoner took the meat from the dog and put it in a handkerchief.

Mrs. Brewer sent for her husband, who followed the prisoner and bought him back to the shop. The prisoner then took the meat from the handkerchief, and said that sooner than be locked up he would pay the double value of the pig's head, but he was given into custody.

In defence the prisoner said he was out with his dog, but as it was dark he did not notice it go into the shop. The animal was only a puppy, about eleven months old. The Bench said they could not believe the prisoner's version of the story and fined him 20s. and 14s. costs, the default being twenty-one days' imprisonment with hard labour.

(11.10.1884)

# THE TRAFFIC IN ENGLISH GIRLS

Last week a journalist interviewed Miss Cox who said:

I am seventeen years of age, and as my mother died when I was about twelve years old, I have since been living with some friends, who have taken care of me. Owing, however, to the gentleman dying about a month ago, I knew that the widow would not be able to keep me, so I looked out for a situation.

I went to the Strand Agency office about two months ago, and paid a shilling for a place to be got for me. While going backwards and forwards there every morning I met Caroline Mountford, and on the 8th of April she told me that she had been referred to a lady in Covent-garden who had engaged her, and who wanted her to get another young girl to go with her. I went round and saw the lady, and she said she thought I should do very nicely, but she wanted us particularly to go away that night.

I agreed to go, and as time was very short I started without letting my brother or any of my relatives know where I was going. As business had been bad with my friends I thought I should like to go where I could earn the most money, though I might have to put up with some little inconvenience.

We got there [Le Havre, France] as described by Caroline Mountford, but I had no idea of the kind of place to which I was going. The lady was very pleasant, and told us that we need not do anything that day, but go upstairs and look over the music, and see what songs we could pick out to sing. We were to go on the first few nights as English village maidens with hats and small baskets of flowers. The other girls were dressed in scarlet low-bosomed dresses, but ours were not made. When we saw at night what sort of a place it was, with all the girls coming, we did not want to go on the stage at all.

The keepers of the place pushed us on and said that we would still have to fulfil our engagement. We went on to the stage the first few nights, as we were forced to do so; but whilst we were on the whole conduct of all around was so shocking and disgraceful that no respectable girl could put up with it, and I should think nothing of the kind is ever seen in England.

The stage on which we had to dance and sing, projects out from one of the sides of a room to the middle, and the men gathered round it quite close. Some men pinched us. When we complained to the manager they said we should have to do what we were wanted to do. Though they were kind to us the first day or two, they were not afterwards but began to blackguard us.

As soon as I saw what sort of place we had unfortunately been decoyed to, I wrote home to my friends, and begged them to try and do something for us as soon as they could, as I was sorry to say that we had "been taken to a gay house." My friends went immediately to one of the London societies for putting down traffic in English girls.

The danger seemed to increase every night, for after the house was shut up a number of men remained. We were made to sit with them and smoke cigars, gamble with them, and toss them for bottles of champagne. There are between forty and fifty beds in the house, I should think…

We were in great danger all the time we were there; and we only signed the statement which we did through fear and threats, and to get away as quickly as we could and have our passage paid back.

(02.05.1885)

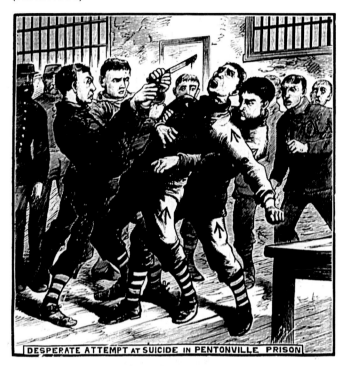

DESPERATE ATTEMPT AT SUICIDE IN PENTONVILLE PRISON

# DESPERATE ATTEMPT AT SUICIDE IN PENTONVILLE PRISON
By an eye witness

We have received from a correspondent a sketch of the scene depicted on our front page, together with a written description of the same. Our correspondent complains, in common with many others, of the harsh treatment and oppressive severity practised on prisoners. He goes on to say:

"In Pentonville Prison there is a large shoe shop, where about one hundred men are employed in making boots for the Metropolitan Police, amongst whom was a man named George Hawks, from Finedon, near Wellington, who was convicted and sentenced, at Northampton, to seven years, about four and a half years ago, for assaulting the police or keepers in a poaching affair. It appears that some time previous he had been in a similar mess, when he was forced by the police to turn Queen's evidence (so he says), which has preyed on his mind a great deal, and for some time past he has been very dejected and depressed. The prisoners are not allowed to speak to anyone, and being all the time subject to most galling tyranny, it makes life a burden.

The other week just as the men were leaving off work and their knives were being collected, this man was seen with both hands up to his throat as though in pain, till a man standing near him saw some blood, and then shouted, 'Look! Don't you see him cutting his throat?' Whereupon three of the men rushed at him just as he was plunging the knife upward in a fearful gash he had made, and he rushed off across the shop shouting that he was innocent, and would not live to do it. Several men followed him and threw him down, and got their hands badly cut in taking the knife from him. They were completely covered with blood, but at last managed to secure him, and get him to the infirmary.

Had it not been for several prisoners he would certainly have done serious injury to others, and have killed himself. He fortunately did not cut any vital part, and is getting out of danger, and when sufficiently recovered he will be taken before one of the directors, perhaps to be sentenced to receive about three dozen lashes, or put in chains for six months, wear a particoloured dress, and perhaps twenty-eight days' bread and water, and lose all his remission! But whatever doctors may say, all who saw the poor fellow were convinced he was out of his mind, and knew not what he did, and as I shall get to know all about it, they may depend on my exposing it.

Many other even worse cases I have witnessed and hope soon to publish in a volume, and I have no doubt the public will be horrified at the cruelty practised in their midst. One of the latest pieces of barbarity is at Chatham and Borstal, where the nightwatchmen have orders to push a lamp through an opening in the cell doors and wake the men up every half hour during the night!"

JOHN D. BAUCUTTE.
"54, Lorne-road, Northampton."

(23.05.1885)

THE CONSTABLE DESCENDING

ATTEMPTED SUICIDE—GALLANT CONDUCT OF A POLICEMAN

## ATTEMPTED SUICIDE – GALLANT CONDUCT OF A POLICEMAN

On Saturday night, last week, just before eight o'clock, an aged man, name unknown, jumped off Chelsea Bridge, falling on to the buttress. He lay there insensible, having injured his head and lost a great deal of blood, and in consequence of there being a low tide he could not be reached from the river, the height of the granite stonework being then about fifteen feet, nor could any aid be at first rendered from the bridge. The utmost excitement prevailed among the people on the bridge, which was crowded with spectators, who were apprehensive that the unfortunate man would fall into the river and be drowned.

At last a rope was procured, and a policeman courageously descended and rescued the man, who was conveyed in a Thames Conservancy boat to Westminster Bridge, and thence to St. Thomas's Hospital, where he died within five minutes after his admission.

(06.06.1885)

## GROSS ASSAULT IN A RAILWAY CARRIAGE

At the Greenwich Police-court, on Friday, John Watkins, twenty-nine, commercial agent, of 80, Penton-place, Newington Butts, was charged with indecently assaulting Miss Fanny Elizabeth Bull, a governess, in a railway carriage on the South-Eastern Railway. Mr. Willis appeared for the prosecution on the part of the railway company; Mr. Forman watched the case in the interest of Miss Bull.

The prosecutrix deposed that she was a governess, and resided with her mother. On Thursday afternoon she returned from Eltham, where she had been teaching, to St. John's, by the South-Eastern Railway. She got into an empty carriage at Eltham, but just as the train was starting the prisoner got in and took his seat at the opposite end.

A few minutes after the train started he came and sat opposite to her, and on arriving at Lee she moved to the other end of the carriage. Nothing occurred until the train left Lee, when the prisoner again came to where she was sitting, and stood up, looking out of window.

Suddenly he seized hold of her, held her down and indecently assaulted her. She struggled to get away, and bit his cheek, and then his hand. She got one hand free, and the communicator being above her she pulled it about two inches, when the prisoner pulled her back. He put both his arms round her, and tried to hold her down. Getting her left arm free, she succeeded in opening the door, and to get out on the footboard. Her right hand was inside by the window, and she was waving her left for the train to stop. The prisoner kept hold of her hand.

The train was pulled up in a few minutes, when she was put into another carriage, and went on to New Cross, where the prisoner was taken into custody.

Mr. Marsham: Did the prisoner say anything to you?

Witness: Nothing; I did not hear him speak.

GROSS · ASSAULT IN A RAILWAY CARRIAGE·

Prisoner: I should like to ask the lady if she could say if I was sober at the time.

Witness: I do not know.

Prisoner: I plead guilty. Is there any use in going on with the case?

Mr Forman asked the magistrate if, under these circumstances, he could deal with the prisoner, and so save the prosecutrix the unhappiness of having to appear at the Old Bailey against him. Mr. Marsham said he should feel it his duty to send the case for trial.

William Thomas Dover, guard on duty with the train in question, said he left Dartford at 4.20.p.m. and on leaving Lee, just past the Hither-green signals, the communicator rang, but at the same time the driver was stopping. On looking out he saw the prosecutrix standing on the continuous footboard of a second-class carriage. He went to her assistance immediately the train stopped, and she made a complaint to him, but not in the presence of the prisoner. He put her in another carriage, and locked the prisoner in, the train then proceeding to St. John's. Here witness put a porter in with him, and went on to New Cross.

Police-constable Wintall, 103 R, deposed to receiving the prisoner into custody. At the station he was asked his name and replied, "Jack," for a long time refusing to give any other description of himself. In his pocket witness found a third-class ticket from Eltham to London Bridge. Other evidence was given of the prisoner being sober.

Mr. Marsham committed him for trial at the Central Criminal Court. He consented to take two sureties in £50, and his own in £100 for his appearance.

(22.08.1885)

*Watkins pleaded guilty and was sentenced to three months with hard labour.*

RECAPTURE

DARING ATTEMPT TO ESCAPE FROM THE HOUSE OF CORRECTION

## ESCAPE AND RECAPTURE OF A PRISONER

At the Clerkenwell Police-court on Wednesday, George Mousley, thirty-eight, a prisoner at the House of Correction, Coldbath Fields, was charged with having committed a breach of prison regulations by escaping from the gaol on Tuesday morning.

Police-constable Bennett, 268 G said Mousley, when he escaped from the prison, was undergoing twelve months' hard labour for felony. On Tuesday morning at half-past eight, witness was on "protection duty" outside the walls of the prison, and while walking up Farringdon-road, he saw the prisoner in the gaol uniform, running along the pavement in the direction of King's Cross. He was running on the side of the road opposite to the prison wall, and witness crossed over, and, after a short chase, captured him.

The prisoner was wearing a portion of a sack tied round his neck, which covered his coat and his convict number. He was bleeding from a cut in his forehead, and he said, "Don't stop me, I am running to the doctor's." The witness told him that he believed he (Mousley) was an escaped prisoner and took him to the King's Cross Police-station.

Further evidence was given by the gaol officials that Mousley was sentenced to twelve months' imprisonment for stealing tools in May last. He was a stonemason. At about half-past eight on Tuesday morning Mousley was engaged in dressing some stones at an outbuilding in the prison yard, at the south side of the gaol. He managed to get out of the building, the door of which was locked, by breaking away some of the iron grating at the window. There was no warder near at the time.

On getting into the yard he scaled two walls – the inner wall, about twelve feet high, and the outer main wall, nearly twenty feet high. This he effected by means of a scaffold-pole which he took from the out-building mentioned, which was undergoing repairs. He jumped from the top of the outer wall on to the pavement of Guildford-street, Clerkenwell, cutting his forehead as he fell. The prisoner, in answer to the charge, said, "I am very sorry; I have been in such trouble about my home. The chance came all of a sudden into my head, and I took it."

Mr. Barlow committed the prisoner for trial at the Central Criminal Court.

(10.10.1885)

## A BURGLAR'S INDISCRETION

At Thames Police-court Joseph Herrman, thirty-two, cook on board the steamship Nemania, was brought up for burglariously entering Sussex House, 32, East India Dock-road, and stealing therefrom a bottle of gin, five dessert forks, and thirteen spoons, value 15s., the property of Edward Bartier, a photographer, of the above address.

A BURGLARS INDISCRETION

AN ANGRY HUSBAND-CHELSEA

The prosecutor said he went to bed on Saturday night at twelve o'clock, when he locked up all the doors except those in the conservatory and library. There was a ladder outside the house. On Sunday morning at seven o'clock he was awakened by his daughter, and on going downstairs found the prisoner asleep on the couch in the breakfast-room, and the bottle of gin and a toy lantern by his side. Witness also missed the forks and spoons. He sent for the police, and they awoke Herrman and took him into custody.

Ellen Bartier, daughter of the prosecutor, said that on Sunday morning, when she came downstairs, she found the gas alight in the kitchen. On going into the breakfast room she found the prisoner lying on the couch asleep. Witness then woke her father up and told him of it. Constable 266 K deposed that on Sunday morning he was called to the house, and found the prisoner asleep. He woke him up, when he said, "If the gin had not been so strong I would not have been here now."

When searched the forks and spoons were found on the prisoner. Sergeant Brown, 2 K, stated that on the previous morning he examined the premises, and found that an entrance had been effected by getting over a wall in Oriental-street into the prisoner's garden, through the conservatory door, and into the library.

Mr. Saunders committed the prisoner for trial.

(17.10.1885)

## AN ANGRY HUSBAND – CHELSEA

On Tuesday last week at the Westminster Police-court, Mr. Romeo Drysdale, forty-seven, gentleman of 145, Church-strret, Chelsea, was charged on a warrant, before Mr. Partridge, with threatening to murder Mr. George Charles Jackson, a surveyor, residing at 8, Oakley-crescent, Chelsea.

The prosecutor stated that at eight o'clock on Sunday morning, he was awakened by hearing a noise in his room. He started up in bed, and found the defendant, buttoned up in a large overcoat, standing over him, with a huge cudgel upraised in a threatening way. Defendant said he would murder him. Believing firmly that he was in the hands of a madman, he made a rush to the window and lifted the sash. Defendant ordered him back, and said that he would not injure him if he laid down. (Laughter.)

Although very frightened – for he believed that his visitor had an attack of delirium tremens, he got into bed again. No sooner had he done so than Mr. Drysdale locked the door and put the key in his pocket, and said, "Now I'll settle you – I'll murder you." Feeling his defenceless position, and terrified by defendant's manner he vaulted out of bed for the second time, jumped on to the dressing-table, and out into the back yard, a drop of 15ft. He then called out to the landlady for assistance. He had given Mr. Drysdale no provocation.

**THROWING A CHILD OUT OF WINDOW.**

He had, however, no vindictive feeling against him and only desired protection.

Defendant asked him whether, during his absence at Brighton recently, he (Jackson) had not slept in his house – in fact in his wife's bedroom. Prosecutor said he certainly remained one night in Mr. Drysdale's house, but he slept in the morning room. He remained talking to Mrs. Drysdale and her sister until two o'clock, expecting the defendant home from Brighton.

Defendant: Nothing of the sort. You knew well enough I could not get from Brighton at that hour – the last train arrives at midnight. You took advantage of my absence and slept in my wife's bedroom.

In answer to Mr. Partridge, who asked what right he had at the house at all in the absence of Mr. Drysdale, Mr. Jackson stated that he had been on very friendly terms with the prosecutor for sixteen years, and had stayed at his house on many occasions – he might say for months at a time.

The defendant said he went to the prosecutor's room to demand an explanation of his conduct, but he was not suffering from delirium tremens, or in any way excited by drink. Prosecutor was evidently alarmed, and, to calm his fears, for the sake of a little conversation, he swore he would not hurt him, and threw his stick on the bed.

Prosecutor: No; I remember it well. (Laughter.) You held it by the middle, clutched in your fist. Vince, one of the warrant officers, proved that he arrested the defendant, who said that he went to have an interview with Jackson, "man to man," Prosecutor, however, was

frightened, and "would not put his hands up." He then directed him to lie down on the bed, so that he could listen to what he (defendant) said.

Mr. Partridge remanded the defendant, who was bailed later in the day, a solicitor who appeared for him stating that a very different complexion would be put on the case when it came before the court again.

(14.11.1885)

*At the next hearing the case was dropped with Mr. Drysdale accepting that his friend and wife had not been engaged in any hanky-panky during his absence.*

## THROWING A CHILD OUT OF A WINDOW

On Wednesday, last week, Dr. Diplock concluded an adjourned inquiry at the Talbot, Clarendon-road, Notting Hill, as to the death of Henry John Base, aged nine months. The mother, Esther Base, is now under remand at the Hammersmith Police-court on a charge of causing the death of the child by throwing it out of a window at 37, Talbot-grove, on Sunday morning.

The evidence given at the first hearing went to show that the mother had suffered from extreme nervous excitement, and that she laboured under a delusion that someone wanted to take away her child.

On the day in question she rose from her seat and threw the child out of the window.

On this occasion additional evidence as to the woman's habits of sobriety were adduced. Fanny Tyler, of 1, St. George's-road, said the mother formerly lodged in her house. She had frequently seen her under the influence of drink. The landlady of 37, Talbot-grove, was also called, and gave similar evidence. Dr. Whitlock said that when he saw the woman on Friday she admitted having been drinking a large amount of gin. She was then suffering from delirium tremens. It also appeared that the woman went to the Talbot on Friday, and threw the child over the bar, saying, "Take care of it, as he is going to murder it."

The jury returned the following verdict: That the child died from the effects of a fall from a window, that it was the act of Esther Base, who, at the time of committing such act, was of unsound mind through the influence of drink.

(19.12.1885)

*The baby, who fell thirty feet, died of a fractured skull. Esther convinced herself that the child had gone to the angels. She was ordered to 'be kept in custody as a criminal lunatic until Her Majesty's pleasure be known'.*

## DEATH FROM THE BITE OF A CAT

On Saturday, last week, Mr. St Clare Bedford, the Coroner for Westminster, held an inquiry at the St. Martin's Vestry Hall, concerning the death of John James Ridley Marwano, aged thirteen years, an errand boy, lately residing with his parents at 6 Hallett's-place, Rosoman-street, Clerkenwell, who died in the Charing Cross Hospital on Thursday from the effects of the bite of a cat, inflicted on September 22nd last.

Mrs. Marwano deposed that on the evening of September 22nd, when her son returned from work, he complained of having been bitten by a cat on the thumb.

THE BITE OF A CAT — DEATH FROM HYDROPHOBIA.

She took him to the Royal Free Hospital in Gray's Inn-road, where the wound was cauterised.

Since then no particular notice was taken of the matter, but when the cold weather set in about a week ago he began to complain of his hand hurting him. Witness then bandaged it up, and on the previous Saturday he said the pain had gone up his arm. On Sunday morning he complained again, and witness said, "never mind, old man; it's only the rheumatics," and that seemed to pacify him.

On the following Tuesday morning his breath seemed very much affected, and the boy expressed a wish to be taken to the hospital, so witness obtained a letter for his admission. When he had been placed in a cab he asked for some water, but when some was shown him he hissed and scratched like a cat. By the coroner – It was a strange cat that bit him, and it had not since been found.

Frances Dickinson, a girl living at 104, Hallett's-place, stated that she was with the deceased at the time he was bitten. The cat, which was a black one, was running along making a peculiar noise, when the deceased caught hold of its tail, and the cat turned around and bit him on the thumb. Witness did not know whose cat it was. It also bit witness's brother at the same time. The animal was not making a noise usually made by cats.

Dr. Charles Freeman, house physician at Charing Cross Hospital, said the deceased was brought there about a quarter past one on Tuesday afternoon, complaining of a pain in the thumb and spasm of the throat. He was unable to swallow, and when blown or breathed on the spasms reappeared. He was taken upstairs and put to bed. He could not drink any water from a cup, although he was able to lap from a saucer or spoon. The case was seen by the senior physician, but the deceased became more violent, and died at a quarter

SUNDAY SCHOOL KISSING GAMES

**FURTHER ACCOUNTS OF 'KISSING GAMES'**

to one on Thursday afternoon, the cause of death being hydrophobia.

By the coroner: It was not a very common thing for people to die from hydrophobia through the bite of a cat, because so few cats went mad; but there were cases on record. Cases of hydrophobia had been known to arise through the bite of a rat. The jury returned a verdict of death from hydrophobia.

(23.01.1886)

## KISSING GAMES

*Although it printed the following story, taken from 'a religious newspaper having a claim to respectability', the IPN was very dubious as to its veracity.*

According to our contemporary, Sunday schools and temperance societies are developing the practice of "kissing games" in an astonishing and alarming degree. These modern Saturnalia we are asked to believe, prove especially attractive to teachers and senior scholars, and amongst the advanced youth of both sexes osculation in its most objectionable form proceeds for hours together…

According to our contemporary, he knows of a Sunday school where "kissing games" go on from six in the evening until twelve at night. He tells us that the Sunday-school orgie, of which he was a reluctant witness – leaving at last in disgust – began with a cancan "to an idiotic song and tune." To quote his own words:

"First the upper and then the lower members of the body were raised and swung about. After this an hour was spent in 'kissing and hissing.' Then came the great treat called 'the Army.' Marching round in pairs, these Sunday school teachers went through a drill in which 'Present arms' and 'Fire a volley' meant embracing and kissing between the sexes. When we state that the male 'teachers' knelt down before their partners to embrace

AN OLD MAN'S AFFECTION FOR HIS DOG

them, and that six 'volleys' were ordered at once, or that kissing in that posture was ordered to continue until the word 'Halt!' from the fugleman, the reason of our departure and strong indignant protest will be evident."

(29.03.1886)

# AN OLD MAN'S AFFECTION FOR HIS DOG

At the Southwark Police-court, the other day, Maurice Day, a feeble-looking old man, who carried a small black dog under his arm, appeared before Mr. Shell on a summons for keeping a dog without a licence.

Police-constable 45 M stated that he saw the dog wandering at large without a muzzle in Barford-street, Bermondsey, and found that it belonged to the defendant, who had no licence for the animal. In answer to the magistrate, the defendant, who burst out crying, said: I've had this little dog eighteen years, and have paid the licence for it as long as I could. I have lately had an attack of paralysis, and have not earned any money, so I have not been able to pay for the licence.

Mr. Shell: Why don't you part with the dog?

Defendant: I don't like to part with it after having it so long. The little dog does nobody any harm.

Mr. Shell: You can't be allowed to keep a dog without paying the duty, however long you may have had it. You are fined 7s. 6d., or seven days. The old man was locked up in default.

Mr. Nairn, Chief Clerk of the Court, has written in reference to this case. He says:

"The fine was paid early on Monday morning, and that letters containing money, and telegrams stating the senders' wish to pay the fine, have been received at this court in great numbers from all parts of the country..."

During the day upwards of thirty ladies and gentlemen attended the court with the object of paying the fine. Amongst the applicants were several ladies and gentlemen of title, one of whom went to the Dog's Home at Battersea and restored the dog to its owner, after paying the licence for the ensuing year.

(05.06.1886)

# DESPERATE STRUGGLE IN A RAILWAY CARRIAGE

Lewis Agerstrom, twenty-eight, and David Chaters, thirty-two, seamen, were brought up, at the Marylebone Police court, on Thursday, last week, for being drunk and damaging a railway carriage to the amount of 20s., the property of the London and North-Western Railway Company. Agerstrom was further charged with assaulting Edward Byrne.

The evidence of Francis Fickle, guard in the employ of the company, was that he had charge of the afternoon express from Liverpool to Euston on Monday, in which was a party of sailors, amongst them being the prisoners. Between Castlethorpe and Wolverton a first-class passenger pulled the communication cord, and the train was stopped. It was then discovered that a violent disturbance had taken place between the sailors and the other passengers in the carriage, and that during the

STRUGGLE IN A RAILWAY CARRIAGE—JACK TARS FIGHTING PROCLIVITIES

WHEELING A CORPSE FROM LONDON TO COLCHESTER

struggle the windows had been broken, the blinds torn down, and the seats besmeared with blood. Byrne, who had been assaulted, and who had a large wound on his forehead, had climbed out of the window while the train was in motion to escape from his assailants, and had to stand on the footboard. The occupants of the carriage were separated and brought on to Euston, where the defendants, who were still drunk, were given into custody.

Mr. De Rutzen said he could not deal with the matter of the damage, as it was committed in Northamptonshire, but for being drunk they would each have to pay 20s., or in default seven days' imprisonment.

(12.06.1886)

## WHEELING A CORPSE FROM LONDON TO COLCHESTER

A young woman named Carrie Dansie, who lately died in the Brompton Hospital, before her death expressed a strong desire to be buried at Great Horkesley, Colchester, her native place. The friend who advised her to go to the hospital, and who promised that she should be buried at Horkesley, being unable to bear the cost of having the body conveyed thither by rail, determined to wheel it down on a truck. Accordingly the body was placed in a decent elm coffin and strapped to a truck, and then the poor man, whose name is Balls, started out on his melancholy journey.

He passed through Brentwood with his burden between six and seven o'clock on the evening of Monday, February 7th. On passing through Chelmsford on February 8th, at midday, his singular load attracted much attention. The poor man looked tired and worn; the coffin was wrapped in oilskin, and there were also on the truck a small bicycle lamp to light his way at night, and several articles of luggage.

The driver of a railway goods van kindly gave him help with the truck for a good distance along the Springfield-road. At Kelvedon the man appears to have given an account of his extraordinary proceeding. He said that he first became acquainted with the deceased about nineteen years ago when passing through Great Horkesley in search of employment. The girl was then three years old, living with her grandparents for whom he worked for a little while. Some time ago she wrote to him in London (they had kept up a correspondence), and told him she was obliged to leave her situation at Lexden to go into Colchester Hospital, and on his advice came to Brompton Hospital, and was for some time a patient there.

He frequently visited her, taking every opportunity of reading to her, and did all he could to comfort her in her declining days. One day she said she hoped that when she died she would not be placed in a pauper's coffin and buried in London, and he told her she should be buried in her native village, and he would make her a coffin. This seemed to give her great comfort.

Last week she died and he kept his promise and made her a coffin. He then went to ascertain the cost of removing her from London to her native village and found it was much more than he could, as a working man, afford to pay, and so in order to keep his promise with the dear child, he had, as work was slack, adopted the somewhat novel plan of taking the body himself in this handcart from London to Horkesley, where he intends seeing his charge interred close by the spot where nineteen years ago he first made the acquaintance of the dear girl now gone to her rest. Balls reached Bergholt on Wednesday, February 9th, and the internment took place the next day.

(05.03.1887)

## THE CONFESSION OF LIPSKI

A conference lasting several hours was held at the Home Office on Saturday afternoon, at which, amongst others, Mr. justice Stephen and Mr. Matthews were present. All the circumstances connected with the case of Lipski were exhaustively discussed, with the result that at a late hour on Saturday, the following letter was forwarded by special messenger to Mr. Haywood, the condemned man's solicitor:-

"Whitehall, August 20th, 1887.

"Sir: With reference to the case of Israel Lipski, I am directed to acquaint you that after full consideration of the circumstances, and of all the representations made by yourself and others on behalf of the prisoner, the Secretary of State sees no reason for advising any interference with the due course of the law.- I am, Sir, your obedient servant,

(Signed) "Geoffrey Lushington."

# THE CONFESSION

On Sunday the prisoner made a full confession to the Rev. S.Singer of the circumstances connected with his crime. It is in the following terms. The statement was at once forwarded to the Home Secretary:-

"I, Israel Lipski, before I appear before God in judgement, desire to speak the whole truth concerning the crime of which I am accused. I will not die with a lie on my lips. I will not let others suffer even in suspicion for my sin. I alone was guilty of the murder of Miriam Angel. I thought the woman had money in her room, so I entered, the door being unlocked and the woman asleep.

I had no thought of violating her, and I swear I never approached her with that object, nor did I wrong her in this way. Miriam Angel awoke before I could search about for money, and cried out; but very softly.

Thereupon I struck her on the head and seized her by the neck and closed her mouth with my hand, so that she should not arouse the attention of those that were about the house. I had been utterly tired of my life, and had bought a penny-worth of aquafortis that morning for the purpose of putting an end to myself. Suddenly I thought of the bottle I had in my pocket, and drew it out and poured some of the contents down her throat. She fainted, and recognising my dangerous position, I took the rest. The bottle was an old one which I had formerly used, and was the same as that which I had taken with me to the oil shop. The quantity of aquafortis I took had no effect on me.

Hearing the voices of people coming upstairs I crawled under the bed. The woman seemed already dead. There was only a very short time from the moment of my entering the room until I was taken away. In the agitation I also fainted. I do not know how it was my arms became abraded. I did not feel it, and was not aware of it. As to the door being locked from the inside, I myself did this immediately after I entered the room, wishing not to be interrupted.

I solemnly declare that Rosenbloom and Schmuss know nothing whatever of the crime of which I have been guilty, and I alone. I implore them to pardon me for having in my despair tried to cast the blame upon them. I also seek the forgiveness of the bereaved husband. I admit that I have had a fair trial, and acknowledge the justice of the sentence that has been passed upon me. I desire to thank Mr. Haywood for his efforts on my behalf, as well as all those who have interested themselves in me during this unhappy time. The confession is made of my own free will, and is written down by Mr. Singer at my request. May God comfort my loving father and mother and may He accept my repentance and my death as an atonement for all my sins.

(Signed) "ISRAEL LIPSKI"
Witness: S.Singer, Minister.
E.S.Milman, Governor of her Majesty's Prison, Newgate.
Sunday, August 21st, 1887.

(27.08.1887)

REMOVING LIPSKI FROM UNDER THE BED

OUR TRUSTWORTHY MAID SERVANTS – MASTER & MISTRESS OUT OF TOWN.

# OUR TRUSTWORTHY MAIDSERVANTS

A droll, but to householders a somewhat disquieting, pendant to the old farce of "High Life Below Stairs" came under the notice of Mr. Paget, at Hammersmith Police-court, on Thursday, when two young women, described as domestic servants, were charged with stealing fifty-five bottles of wine, a large quantity of cigars, and other articles, the property of their employer, a solicitor, whose private residence is in the Uxbridge-road.

This gentleman and his wife had gone into the country for the autumnal holidays, leaving their house and their four children in the charge of two female servants, on whose honesty and fidelity, it is to be presumed, they had every reason to rely.

Still the solicitor's wife appears to have suffered from some uneasiness of mind with regard to her olive-branches in London, so she wrote to a 'lady friend in the metropolis, who, acting on the suggestion made to her, paid a visit to the house in the Uxbridge-road, just to see how things were going on.

It was on the evening of the 28th September that the lady knocked at the door; and she was surprised to find the house in apparent darkness. One of the servants, who seemed considerably alarmed at her appearance, admitted the lady, who announced her intention of remaining on the premises all night. The girl who had opened the door continued to reiterate that the house was "all right." Two of the children were in bed and two downstairs. The lady went up to the bed-room of the solicitor's wife, and found the door locked; there was a light inside. She then entered a spare bedroom and discovered a number of empty bottles. Subsequently one of the servants sent up the key of her mistress's bed-room, and on entrance being effected thereto the gas was found to be burning, and the dresses of the lady of the house were beheld lying about in the wildest confusion imaginable.

Neither of the two servants were completely attired, and the natural inference from their state of partial disarray was that they were engaged in the merry diversion of robing themselves in their mistress's garments at the time when they were disturbed. The house, otherwise, was found to be in a state of extreme disorder, and the children had been sadly neglected. While these disagreeable facts were being bought to light, the two hussies who had been getting up so exemplary an interlude of "Low Life Above Stairs" contrived to complete their own toilettes and decamp, but were subsequently taken into custody.

When the solicitor's wife returned to the Uxbridge-road, she found that the house had been ransacked from top to bottom, and every drawer and box opened. The door of the wine-cellar had been forced, and large quantities of wine and cigars abstracted. It stands to reason that these two unfaithful baggages could not have drunk fifty-five bottles of wine between them and smoked all the cigars that were missed. They must have had partakers in their revelry and fellow-roysters in their tippling-bouts; and of the probable character of these boon companions a significant inkling is given in the circumstances that the plundered lady found a couple of skeleton keys in her basket.

(15.10.1887)

# THE CHAMPION SHAVER

On Tuesday night at 418 King's-road, Chelsea, an extraordinary shaving match against time was decided. Teddy Wick, the champion barber, being backed to shave 50 persons in 60 minutes for £15 a-side. He actually shaved 77 in 59 min. 53 sec., and thus won the stakes.

In the first quarter of an hour he disposed of 21 men; in the second 14; in the third 19; and in the last 14 min. 53 sec. he put on a spurt and finished off 23. This feat beats a previous record of 60 odd. Three chairs were in constant use, and Teddy plied in succession three razors.

The "subjects" were customers, who eagerly availed themselves of a free shave and a cigar. Some of them were particularly stubbly about the chin, but, seemingly, that made no difference to the expert barber. Wick is a young, smart, under-sized man, and for two years he has been the acknowledged champion, having in a match against all comers won, shaving 40 men in 50 min.; and on another occasion he came off victor in a blindfold competition.

His latest achievement caused great excitement in Chelsea, and was witnessed by as many persons as his small premises could accommodate. Ned Hubbard, the champion skittle-player was referee; T. Pitcher, ex-champion roller skater, and Mr. W. Eastern acted as timekeepers; and J. Markey, champion barber of Fulham, lathered the sitters. Teddy Wick declares that he is ready to defend his title, and he issues the following manifesto: "To show I mean business, I will give the man or woman who can beat me my silver medal, won by me in the 'Open to the World Competition.' This challenge is open to the world: Twelve men's hair cut, twenty men shaved, with two hands; six men to be shaved, barbers to be blindfolded; and six men shaved one-handed, the left hand to be tied behind, for £15, £50, or £100 a-side

(22.10.1887)

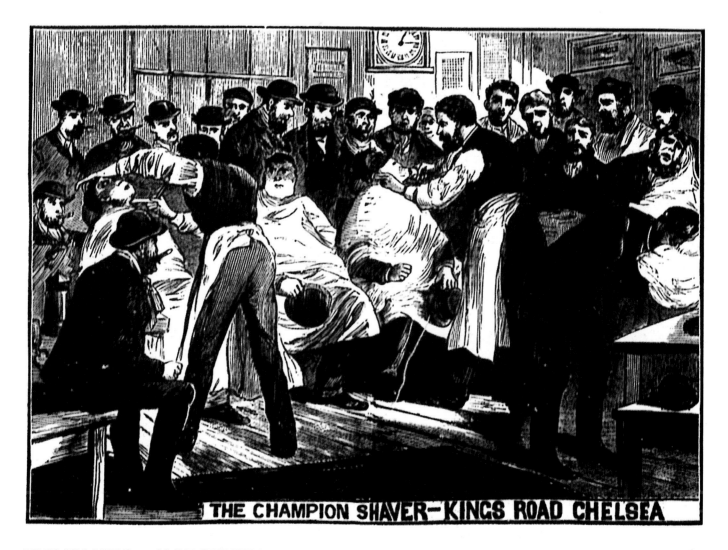

THE CHAMPION SHAVER-KINGS ROAD CHELSEA

## BICYCLISTS v. HORSEMEN

On Saturday last, at the Agricultural Hall, Islington, this contest was bought to a conclusion. The terms of the match were that W.M.Woodside and Richard Howell, on bicycles, should ride against Marve Bardsley and Broncho Charley, on an unlimited number of horses, for six days, the hours of riding being restricted to eight hours per day, and only one competitor on each side to be on the track at the same time.

Throughout the week the contest was of an exciting character, neither side being able to gain a great advantage. The scores on the Friday night were:- Horsemen, 674 miles; bicyclists, 673 miles, 1,320 yards, the cowboys thus having a lead of a quarter of a mile.

From an early hour in the afternoon crowds poured into the building, until at half-past eight there must have been at least twenty thousand spectators. The cowboys had evidently saved some of their fastest mounts for the last day's work, and riding at a tremendous pace they gained hour by hour, until at the forty-sixth hour they had an advantage of one mile 1,100 yards, the distance covered by the leaders being 779 miles.

As the end approached the interest culminated, and amidst a scene of wild excitement the cowboys were hailed the winners by two miles 375 yards, the final score being – cowboys, 814 miles 1,255 yards; bicyclists, 812 miles 880 yards.

(10.11.1887)

HORSE AND BICYCLE CONTEST AT THE AGRICULTURAL HALL

SCENE AT A LONDON EVICTION

## SCENE AT A LONDON EVICTION

At the Marylebone Police-court last week, William Gay, twenty-eight, a brass-finisher of 63, Willes-road, Kentish-town, was charged with wilfully damaging property belonging to James Fowler, also with assaulting Sergeant Carden 11 D, warrant-officer and Constable Giles 93 Y.

Sergeant Carden said he went to the house, 63, Willes-road on Thursday, in last week, to execute a magistrate's ejectment warrant against the prisoner. He and Constable Foyle had got a portion of the furniture into the street when the prisoner came home, and, entering the room, said, "I suppose I may as well begin to move something." At the same time he picked up the tongs, as witness thought to pack them up. Instead,

however, of doing that, he went to the window and struck the sash three or four blows, breaking both the glass and frames.

Witness went to catch hold of the prisoner's shoulders, but missed his right shoulder. The prisoner aimed a blow at the witness with the tongs, but he warded it off. The prisoner then kicked witness on the side of his knee, and his leg went from under him. Witness again grasped hold of the prisoner, and after a struggle he fell. The prisoner was on top of him, and seizing witness's hair with one hand he pummelled at his face with the other, and continued to do so until Constable Foyle pulled him off.

By the magistrate: Witness had been incapacitated

from duty ever since. (The sergeant's face was badly disfigured, and he was only able to walk with the aid of sticks.) Constable Foyle, assistant warrant officer, corroborated, and said when he pulled the prisoner off he was knocked down. Constable Giles, 93 Y, came up, and they got the prisoner out of the house. When in street the prisoner threw witness down and dealt Giles a severe blow on the face.

Sarah Fowler, the landlady, said the prisoner had lodged in her house, and owed six weeks' rent. She got an ejectment from Marylebone Police-court. Which the warrant officers executed on the day in question. Dr. Kirby, divisional surgeon, said Sergeant Carden was badly hurt. His eye was much swollen and disfigured, and his head bruised in several parts. His knee was also severely injured. It would be quite two or three weeks before he would be fir for duty, and he ought then not to be out.

Mr. F. Palmer, solicitor for the prisoner, said his client was very sorry for the injury he had done to Sergeant Carden, who was deservedly held in high esteem by the court. The prisoner had a sick child and a delicate wife, and as the officers would not give him time to get a van he lost his temper, but never intended doing the injury which had followed. He called witnesses showing that he had a good character.

Mr. Newton said that he could not conceive of a worse case. The officer of this court went to execute the order of the magistrate, and because he would not wait for two or three hours he was assaulted in a brutal manner. He sentenced him to three months' imprisonment. There was a scene in court amongst the prisoner's friends, and Mr. Palmer appealed to the magistrate to reduce the sentence. Mr. Newton refused, and said the officers of the court must be protected, or there would be an end of society.

(05.05.1888)

# A WOMAN HANGING BY HER TEETH FROM THE CAR OF A BALLOON

Our engraving represents a performance of an exceptional character. A female acrobat has ascended more than once from the grounds of the Crystal Palace hanging from a horizontal bar attached to the car of a balloon, as shown in our picture.

Last week in the House of Commons Mr. R. Smith asked the Home Secretary whether his attention had been drawn to the performances on Whit Monday at the Crystal Palace of a female aeronaut, who ascended some mile and a half into the air, hanging to a balloon by her teeth; and whether he was prepared to take any steps in the suppression of such exhibitions.

Mr. Matthews said he had seen the account of this performance, but he was informed that the law did not prohibit public performances on account of their danger to adult performers. He had no power to interfere. The law left this matter to the good taste and feelings of the community, which were always sufficient

to correct any unseemly exhibitions. He understood that the danger in this case was more imaginary than real, as the woman was suspended from the car.

(16.06.1888)

THE ASCENT OF LEONA DARE FROM A BALOON AT THE C. PALACE

# EXTRAORDINARY HOAX AT TOTTENHAM

On Thursday at the Edmonton Petty sessions, before Mr. Latham and other divisional justices, Thomas Pracy, fifteen, of 27, Halefield-road, Tottenham; and Walter Scott, nine, of 23, Burlington-road, Tottenham, were charged with stealing a quantity of rhubarb from an enclosed market-garden, the property of Thomas Hollington, of the Hale Farm, Tottenham.

Complainant said that on Monday he received information that between seventy and eighty persons were in his nine-acre field of rhubarb, clearing away the contents. He at once started for the police-station, but met an officer on the way. They proceeded to the field, and there they found about seventy people – men, women, girls, and boys – pulling the rhubarb as fast as they could. Witness estimated that at that time at least forty tons of rhubarb, valued at £40, had been taken away, and a large quantity had been destroyed by being broken or trodden upon. He ascertained that the robbery and destruction of his property had then been going on for about an hour and a half.

On his appearance there was a general stampede, but the constable arrested the defendants with a quantity of rhubarb in their possession. An immense quantity had been thrown into the stream running close to the fence of the field, and mothers and fathers had stood in the brook to receive the rhubarb as it was put over the fence by their children.

# EXTRAORDINARY HOAX AT TOTTENHAM

The following is the explanation of the affair, and shows that a cruel hoax was perpetrated. The field is near the Coleraine-park Schools of the Tottenham School Board, and on Monday a well-dressed man accosted a number of youngsters returning from their morning studies at these schools, and made them believe that he was Mr. Hollington. He inquired if they knew his rhubarb field, and received a chorus of replies in the affirmative. He then told them that the rhubarb season was over, and that they might take away as much as they liked, as he wanted to clear the ground.

The terms of this kindly offer very quickly spread, and in an incredibly brief period a swarm of men, women, and children were in the field gathering the rhubarb. Perambulators, pails, sacks, baskets, and a variety of other receptacles were employed to carry it away, and in less than an hour a splendid field of rhubarb, ready for market, had practically been laid waste. A vast quantity of rhubarb was thrown into the brook mentioned, and a gang of men in the service of the Local Board were sent to clear the obstruction to prevent a flood.

The defendants, who said they were told that the rhubarb had been given away, and that a man stood in the ditch to help boys over the fence, were remanded on 20s. bail to enable the police to endeavour to discover the inciter of the outrage.

(30.06.1888)

## LARRY DONOVAN'S FATAL LEAP

The inquest on the body of Larry Donovan, who has performed some extraordinary feats of jumping from great heights in America, and who lost his life from leaping from Hungerford-bridge, Charing-cross, was held on Monday before Deputy-coroner Wood, at the Brown Bear, High-street, Deptford.

William Cook, of Angel-court, Strand, identified the deceased whom he had known for about two months. His principal occupation was diving, but he did not know whether he got paid for it. He should say his age was about twenty-eight. He had been badly off most of the time the witness had known him.

About two o'clock on Tuesday morning last witness met deceased casually outside Charing-cross Railway Station, where he was accompanied by about twenty people. He (Donovan) said that he had a match on at Brighton to dive against another man off Brighton Pier, and he added that he was going to show them that he could do it. Accompanied by the crowd he went down Villiers-street and on to Hungerford-bridge. He (witness) saw no policeman about, and it was high tide. He walked along the bridge about thirty yards, took off his hat and coat, got over the parapet, and jumped in. When he rose to the surface – in a few seconds – he swam about thirty yards in the direction of Cleopatra's Needle steps, which were about hundred yards from the bridge, and then sank. He did not cry out or throw up his arms, but sank like a stone.

By this time a policeman had arrived on the Embankment, but he could not say whether he witnessed the occurrence. He had seen deceased drunk on one occasion at his house. He was sober when he dived off the bridge. A waterman named Harris stated that early on Saturday morning while he was in his boat between Millwall and St. George's Stairs, Deptford, he picked the deceased's body up and towed it ashore, where it was removed to the mortuary. The deceased had his boots on but was minus his coat and hat.

The coroner's officer deposed to searching the body and finding the portion of an American directory thereon. There was a slight bruise on the deceased's right knee, but no other marks of violence. The knees of his trousers were both missing. He did not know who took charge of the hat and coat, but the hat had since been found on Hungerford-bridge.

The Coroner in summing up referred to the dangerous experiments now being made, and said it was a terrible state of affairs, but it was a difficult thing to see how to stop them when they were paid for. A verdict that deceased was killed by jumping into the Thames was returned.

(18.08.1888)

## TRAGEDY IN WHITECHAPEL

### A WOMAN STABBED IN THIRTY-NINE PLACES

About ten minutes to five o'clock on Tuesday morning a man, who lives at 47, George-yard-buildings, Whitechapel, was coming downstairs to go to work when he discovered the body of a woman lying in a pool of blood on the first-floor landing.

Reeves at once called in Constable Barrett, 26 H, who was on his beat in the vicinity of George-yard, and Dr. Keleene, of Brick-lane, was communicated with, and promptly arrived. He made an examination of the woman, and pronounced life extinct, giving it as his opinion that she had been brutally murdered, there being knife wounds on her breast, stomach, and abdomen. There were thirty-nine wounds in various parts of the body, which was that of a woman apparently between thirty-five and forty years of age, about five foot three inches in height, complexion and hair dark; with a dark green skirt, a brown petticoat, a long black jacket, and a black bonnet.

The woman was not known to any of the occupants of the tenements on the landing on which the deceased was found, and no disturbance of any kind was heard during the night. The body was removed to Whitechapel mortuary…

FATAL LEAP OF THE CHAMPION DIVER.

Dr. Timothy Robert Keleene, 28 Brick-lane stated that he was called to the deceased and found her dead. He examined the body and found thirty-nine punctured wounds. There were no less than nine in the throat and seventeen in the breast. She appeared to have been dead three hours. The body was well nourished. He had since made a post-mortem examination, and found the left lung penetrated in five places and the right lung in two places. The heart had been penetrated but only in one place – otherwise it was quite healthy. The liver was healthy, but penetrated in five places, and the spleen was penetrated in two places. The stomach was penetrated in six places. In the witness's opinion the wounds were not inflicted with the same instrument, there being a deep wound in the breast from some long, strong instrument, while most of the others were done, apparently, with a penknife. The large wound could have been caused by a sword-

Inquiries were at once set on foot by the police and military authorities, with the result that it is stated two soldiers have been placed under military arrest at the Tower. The authorities decline to give their names unless some definite charge is formulated. The two soldiers are said to belong to the Guards.

A perplexing feature in connection with the outrage is the number of injuries on the young woman's body. That the stabs were from a weapon shaped like a bayonet is almost established beyond doubt. The wound over the heart was alone sufficient to kill, and death must have occurred as soon as that was inflicted. Unless the perpetrator was a madman, or suffering to an unusual extent from drink delirium, no tangible explanation can be given of the reason for inflicting the other thirty-eight injuries, some of which almost seem as if they were due to thrusts and cuts from a penknife.

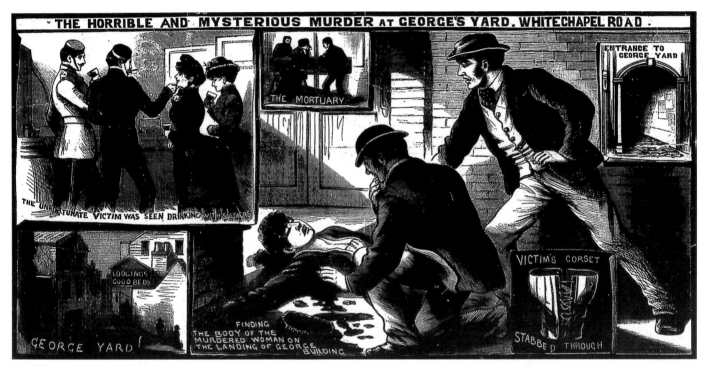

"THE HORRIBLE AND MYSTERIOUS MURDER AT GEORGE'S YARD, WHITECHAPEL ROAD."

bayonet or dagger. It was impossible for the whole of the wounds to be self-inflicted. Death was due to the loss of blood consequent on the injuries.

## TWO ARRESTS AT THE TOWER

The case is in certain respects one of a very puzzling character, owing to the fact that so many stab wounds were inflicted, and that no cries were heard, although the poor woman was on some stone steps, close to the doors of small rooms wherein several separate families resided.

It now appears that on the night of Bank holiday there were several soldiers in the neighbourhood, some of whom were seen drinking in the Princess Alice – two minutes walk from George-yard-buildings – and other taverns near. With these soldiers were the deceased and another woman, the latter being known in the district as "Megg" and "Pearly Poll". One of these men was a private, the other a corporal. It has been ascertained that only corporals and sergeants are allowed to wear side-arms when on leave. This fact, of course, narrows the issue as to the possible identity of the assailant – presuming he was a soldier.

On the other hand, if the lesser wounds were given before the one fatal injury the cries of the deceased must have been heard by those who, at the time of the outrage, were sleeping within a few yards of the spot where the deed was committed.

(18.08.1888)

*Both guardsmen were cleared following an inspection of their clothes and bayonets.*

*The murder of Martha Turner took place just two weeks before what modern-day Ripperologists consider to be his first crime, the murder of Polly Nicholls on 31st August. As was the case with the Ripper's victims, nobody ever stood trial for the killing of Martha Turner. The very last paragraph of the IPN report makes for interesting reading:*

Mrs. Hewitt remarked that early in the evening she did hear a single cry of "Murder." It echoed through the building, but did not emanate from there. "But," explained Mr. and Mrs. Hewitt, in a breath, "the district round here is quite rough, and cries of 'Murder' are of frequent, if not nightly occurrence in the district."

# THE MURDER IN WHITECHAPEL

*The Ripper murders took up more column inches than any other story in the history of the IPN. Some of the front pages have been used extensively in films and books about the atrocities. The illustrations here are amongst the lesser-known, and the stories are included, as much for their revelations about the lives of abject poverty endured by the victims, as they are for the factual details of the murders. The texts are those read by the Victorian public and maybe the perpetrator him/herself.*

At a quarter to four on Friday morning Police-constable Neil was on his beat in Buck's-row, Thames-street, Whitechapel, when his attention was attracted to the body of a woman lying on the pavement close to the

arrived on the scene. He found the body lying on its back across the gateway, and the briskest possible examination was sufficient to prove that life was extinct. Death had not long ensued, because the extremities were still warm. With the assistance of Police-sergeant Kirby and Police-constable Thane, the body was removed to the Whitechapel-road mortuary, and it was not until the unfortunate woman's clothes were removed that the horrible nature of the attack which had been made upon her transpired.

It was then discovered that in addition to the gash in her throat, which had severely severed the head from the body, the lower part of the abdomen had been ripped up, and the bowels were protruding. The abdominal wall, the whole length of the body, had been cut open, and on either side were two incised wounds almost as severe as the centre one. They reached from

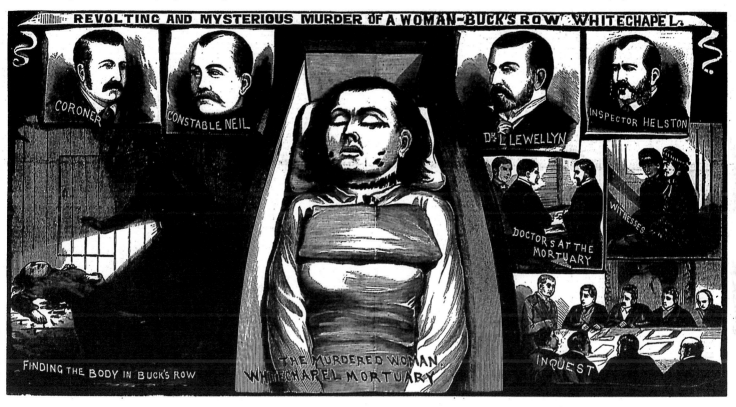

REVOLTING AND MYSTERIOUS MURDER OF A WOMAN~BUCK'S ROW WHITECHAPEL

CORONER — CONSTABLE NEIL — Dr L LEWELLYN — INSPECTOR HELSTON — WITNESSES — DOCTORS AT THE MORTUARY

FINDING THE BODY IN BUCK'S ROW — THE MURDERED WOMAN. WHITECHAPEL MORTUARY — INQUEST

door of the stable-yard in connection with Essex Wharf.

Bucks-row, like many other minor thoroughfares in this and similar neighbourhoods, is not overburdened with gas lamps, and in the dim light the constable at first thought that the woman had fallen down in a drunken stupor and was sleeping off the effects of a night's debauch. With the aid of the light from his bullseye lantern Neil at once perceived that the woman had been the victim of some horrible outrage. Her livid face was stained with blood and her throat cut from ear to ear.

The constable at once alarmed the people living in the house next to the stable-yard, occupied by a carter named Green and his family, and also knocked up Mr. Walter Perkins, the resident manager of the Essex Wharf, on the opposite side of the road, which is very narrow at this point. Neither Mr. Perkins nor any member of the Green family, although the latter were sleeping within a few yards of where the body was discovered, had heard any sound of a struggle.

Dr. Llewellyn, who lives only a short distance away in Whitechapel-road, was at once sent for and promptly

the lower part of the abdomen to the breast-bone. The instrument with which the wounds were inflicted must have been not only of the sharpness of a razor, but used with considerable ferocity.

The murdered woman is about forty-five years of age, and 5ft. 2in. in height. She had a dark complexion, brown eyes, and brown hair, turning grey. At the time of her death she was wearing a brown Ulster fastened with seven large metal buttons with the figure of a horse and a man standing by its side stamped thereon. She had a brown linsey frock and a grey woollen petticoat with flannel underclothing, close-ribbed brown stays, black woollen stockings, side-spring boots, black straw bonnet trimmed with black velvet. The mark "Lambeth Workhouse – P.R." was found stamped on the petticoat bands, and a hope is entertained that by this deceased's identity may be discovered. A photograph of the body has been taken, and this will be circulated amongst the workhouse officials.

(08.09.1888)

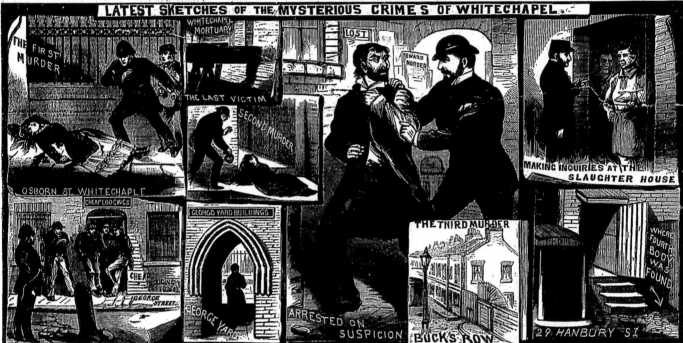

## ANOTHER MURDER IN WHITECHAPEL

A FOURTH VICTIM OF AN UNKNOWN ASSASSIN.
FIENDISH MUTILATION OF A WOMAN'S BODY

*Annie Chapman was probably the second Ripper victim, not the fourth.*

A fourth murder, of a most brutal nature, has been committed in Whitechapel. At a spot only a very few hundred yards from where the mangled body of the poor woman Nicholls was found, the body of another woman, mutilated and horribly disfigured, was found at half-past five on Saturday morning. She was lying in the back yard of 20, Hanbury-street, Spitalfields, a house occupied by Mr. Richardson, a packing-case maker.

As late as five o'clock in the morning it is said the woman was drinking in a public-house near at hand called the Three Bells. Near the body was discovered a rough piece of iron sharpened like a knife. The wounds upon the poor woman were more fearful than those found upon the body of the woman Nicholls, who was buried on Thursday. The throat was cut in a most horrible manner and the stomach terribly mutilated…

The victim was lying on her back with her legs outstretched. Her throat was cut from ear to ear. Her clothes were pushed up above her waist and her legs bare. The abdomen was exposed, the woman having been ripped up from groin to breast-bone, as before. Not only this, but the viscera had been pulled out and scattered in all directions, the heart and liver being placed behind her head and the remainder along her side. No more horrible sight ever met a human eye, for she was covered with blood and lying in a pool of it.

### THE INQUEST

Timothy Donovan, 35, Dorset-street, Spitalfields, deputy of the common lodging-house, said: I identify the body at the mortuary as that of a woman who has lodged in my place. She had lived there for four months, but was not at No. 35 last week, until the Friday.

Afterwards at about two or three o'clock, she asked me to allow her to go into the kitchen. I consented, and did not see her until about a quarter to two on Saturday morning. At this time I was sitting in the office and I saw deceased go into the kitchen. Deceased afterwards came upstairs, saying she had not sufficient money for a bed, and adding; "Don't let it; I shan't be long before I am in." the bed she spoke of was the one she usually occupied.

The deceased left the house, and I did not see which way she turned, but I believe the watchman did. She had had enough to drink when I last saw her, but she could walk straight. She was generally the worse for drink on Saturdays, but not on other days. When she left the lodging-house on Saturday morning I said to her. "You can find money for beer, but not for your bed." She replied that she had only been to the top of the street, to the Ringers public-house. I saw deceased with no man that night. I could not say whether deceased walked the streets. She used to come and stay at the lodging-house on Saturday with a man of soldierly appearance, and who is said to be a pensioner. She has come at other times with other men, and I have refused to allow her to have a bed.

The Coroner: A woman has only one husband at your place?

Donovan: The pensioner told me not to let her have a bed with any other man. She did not come to my place with any man on Friday night. As a rule she occupied No.29 bed by herself.

(15.09.1888)

# THE WHITECHAPEL MURDERS

At the inquest of Mrs. Annie Chapman, who was found dead in the yard of the house 29, Hanbury-street, Whitechapel, her body dreadfully cut and mutilated, early on the morning of Saturday, the 8th last. The following further evidence was called.

Eliza Cooper: I am a cooper and lodge in Dorset-street, Spitalfields. Have done so for the last five months. I know the deceased and had a quarrel with her on the Tuesday before she was murdered. The quarrel arose in this way.

On the previous Saturday she brought Mr. Stanley into the house where I lodged in Dorset-street, and coming into the kitchen asked the people to give her some soap. They told her to ask "Liza" - meaning me. She came to me, and I opened the locker and gave her some. She gave it to Stanley, who went outside and washed himself in the lavatory. When she came back I asked for the soap, but she did not return it. She said, "I will see you by and bye." Mr. Stanley gave her two shillings, and paid for her bed for two nights. I saw no more of her that night.

On the following Thursday I saw her in the kitchen of the lodging-house. I said, "Perhaps you will return my soap." She threw a halfpenny on the table, and said, "Go and get a halfpennyworth of soap." We got quarrelling over this piece of soap, and we went out to the Ringers public-house and continued to quarrel. She slapped my face and said, "Think yourself lucky I don't do more." I struck her in the left eye, I believe, and then in the chest. I afterwards saw that the blow I gave her had marked her face.

When was the last time you saw her alive?

On the Thursday night, in the Ringers.

Was she wearing rings?

Yes, she was wearing three rings on the middle finger of the left hand. They were all brass.

Had she ever a gold wedding ring to your knowledge?

No, not since I have known her. I have known her about fifteen months. I know she associated with Stanley, "Harry the Hawker," and several others.

The Foreman: Are there any of these with whom she associated missing?

I could not tell.

A Juryman: Was she on the same relations with them as she was with Stanley?

No, sir. She used to bring them casually into the lodging-house.

(29.09.1888)

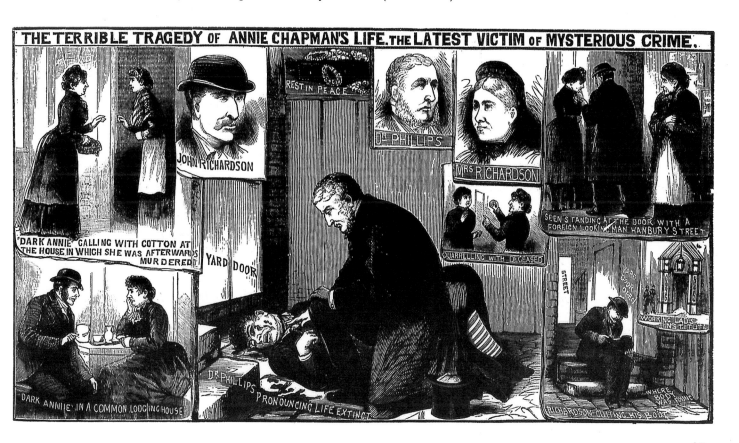

# POLICE NEWS
## LAW COURTS AND WEEKLY RECORD

THE BERNER ST VICTIM.

INSPECTOR REID

INQUEST ON FIFTH VICTIM AT ST GEORGES IN THE EAST.

## TWO MORE WHITECHAPEL HORRORS. WHEN WILL THE MURDERER BE CAPTURED?

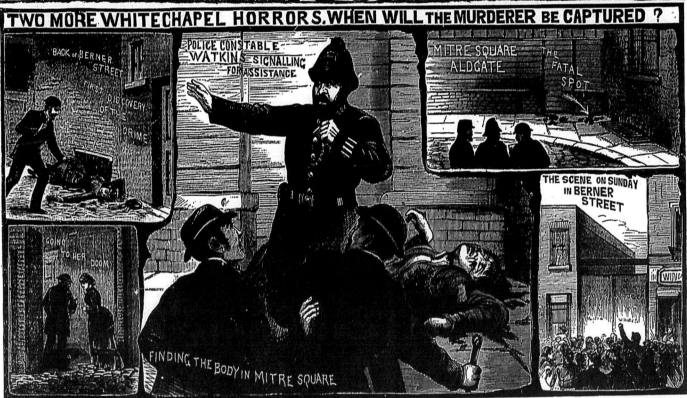

BACK OF BERNER STREET

FIRST DISCOVERY OF THE CRIME

POLICE CONSTABLE WATKINS SIGNALLING FOR ASSISTANCE

MITRE SQUARE ALDGATE

THE FATAL SPOT

GOING TO HER DOOM

FINDING THE BODY IN MITRE SQUARE

THE SCENE ON SUNDAY IN BERNER STREET

EXTERIOR OF THE GATE

THE FIFTH VICTIM OF THE WHITECHAPEL FIEND.

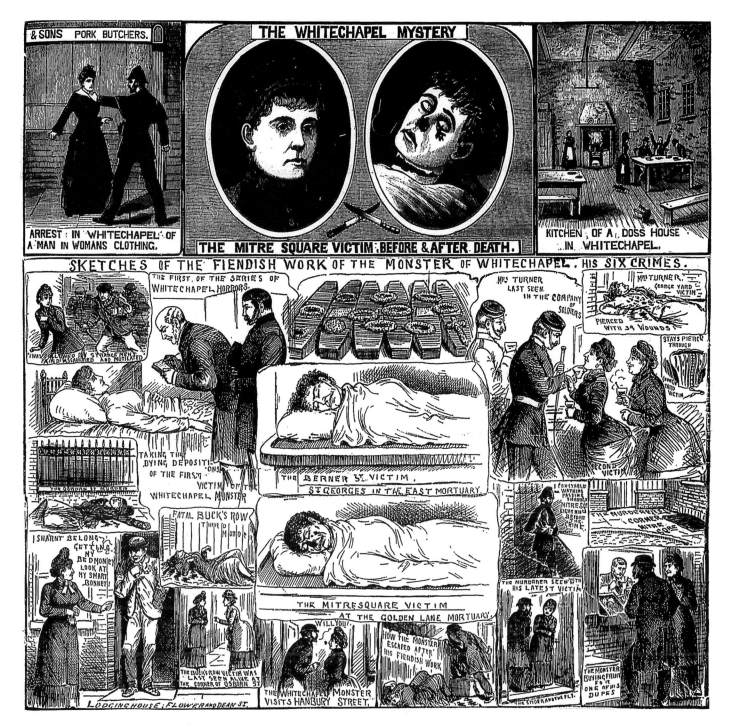

# THE EAST END HORRORS

*Details from the report on a night of double murder. The Ripper had probably been disturbed whilst attacking Elizabeth Stride in Berner Street and set out to satisfy his lust for blood on a second victim.*

Dr. Gordon Brown, sergeant to the City of London Police force, said that he reached Mitre-square at eighteen minutes past two, and found the body [of Kate Eddowes] as described by Police-constable Watkins, with the arms by the side, as if they had fallen there. All the lower part of the body was exposed, and destitute of underclothing. There was a great disfigurement of the face; the throat was cut across. The intestines were drawn out to a large extent and placed over the right shoulder – a piece about two feet in length was quite detached from the body and placed between the left hand and the body, apparently by design. The lobe of the right ear was cut obliquely through.

There was a quantity of clotted blood on the pavement on the left side of the body above the shoulder, and fluid blood – coloured serum which had flowed under the neck – by the right shoulder, the pavement sloping in that direction. The body was quite warm, and *rigor mortis* had not set in, showing that death had occurred within half an hour.

Mr. Crawford: Can you speak with certainty as to that?

Witness: Yes; between thirty and forty minutes – Continuing witness said he looked for superficial bruises and saw none. There was no blood or secretion on the thighs or the lower part of the body. There was no spurting of blood upon the bricks or pavement around; and no marks of blood below the middle of the body.

On Sunday afternoon he made a post-mortem examination and found that the left kidney and portions of the womb had been taken away.

(13.10.1888)

## THE WHITECHAPEL MURDERS

No person is now under detention at either of the metropolitan police-stations in connection with the Whitechapel murders.

SIR CHARLES WARREN'S BLOODHOUNDS LOST

Sir Charles Warren's bloodhounds were out for practice at Tooting on Thursday morning, and were lost. Telegrams were dispatched to all the Metropolitan Police-stations, stating that if seen anywhere information was to be immediately sent to Scotland-yard.

AN EXTRAORDINARY PARCEL

Mr. Lusk, the president of the Whitechapel Vigilance Committee, has received by parcel post a cardboard box containing what has been pronounced by a competent medical authority to be half of the left kidney of an adult human being, and a letter, dated from "Hell" stating, with illiterate brutality, that the half-kidney was a moiety of that taken from Catherine Eddowes, and that the other half had been fried and eaten by the writer. The box, with its contents, has been handed over to the detectives at Leman-street Police-station…

A HOUSE-TO-HOUSE SEARCH

In accordance with the decision of Sir Charles Warren, a body of policemen in plain clothes were on Thursday engaged in making a house-to-house search in the district of the recent murders. No clue to the murderer has, however, been obtained so far.

Several suspected localities are being watched night and day, and indeed it may be said that within a wide area around the scene of the murders there is scarcely a reed of ground that is not under surveillance. The widespread terror prevailing among the class from whom the murderer selected his victim is evidenced by their absence at night from the streets in the vicinity.

(27.10.1888)

## THE WHITECHAPEL MURDER

*Both the public and press were clamouring for an arrest following the butchering of the remains of Mary Kelly.*

During Monday several arrests were made, but after a short examination in all the cases the persons were set at liberty, as it was felt certain they had no connection with the crime. In the Holborn casual ward, on Tuesday, the police arrested a man who gave the name of Thomas Murphy. He was taken by the police to the station at Frederick-street, King's-cross-road, where, on being searched, he was found to have in his possession a somewhat formidable knife with a blade about ten inches long. He was therefore detained in custody on suspicion, and the police proceeded to make inquiries into the truth of his statements. The task was rendered very difficult by the confused and contradictory accounts which Murphy gave of himself. He was detained some time.

Two or three men were arrested during Tuesday night and on Wednesday under circumstances considered suspicious, but in no case did the detention last more than a few hours. Each arrest caused great local excitement, and in connection with one case the whole neighbourhood was in the wildest uproar for a considerable time. The tumult had the customary origin. A man stared into the face of a woman on Whitechapel-road, and she at once screamed out that he was "Jack the Ripper." The unfortunate man was immediately surrounded by an excited and threatening crowd, from which he was rescued with some difficulty by the police. He was taken under a strong escort to the Commercial-street Police-station, followed by an enormous mob of men and women shouting and screaming at him in the most extraordinary manner.

At the police-station the man proved to be a German, unable to speak a word of English. He explained through an interpreter that he arrived in London from Germany on Tuesday and was to leave for America immediately, and confirmation of this statement having been obtained he was set at liberty.

About half-past one on Tuesday morning, some young men watching some premises in Spital-square noticed a man talking to a young woman and overheard him asking her to accompany him. She consented. As they were walking away a constable stopped them and took the man to the Commercial-street Police-station. At a quarter-past three a man was arrested in the Mile-end-road and taken to the Leman-street Police-station. Both prisoners were later on set at liberty.

An arrest has been made at Dover in connection with the Whitechapel murders. A suspicious-looking character was seen near the railway station, and as he answered the description given of the murderer he was taken into custody but afterwards released.

The work of the police has been constantly hampered at times by the agents of private inquiry officers, who, to obtain the offered reward, take upon themselves to follow up what they consider "clues" many of which are in the highest degree absurd. Some of these people have even gone so far as deliberately to present themselves as police-officers, an offence rendering them liable to criminal prosecution under the criminal law.

Several tradesmen in the Whitechapel district, especially those who, like McCarthy, have been mentioned in the newspapers in connection with the last murder, have received anonymous threatening letters of the vilest character.

## NOT HEARD AT THE INQUEST

The following statement has been made by George Hutchinson, a labourer:-

"At twelve o'clock on Friday morning I came down Whitechapel-road into Commercial-street. As I passed Thrawl-street I passed a man standing at the corner of the street, and as I went towards Flower and Dean-street I met the woman Kelly, whom I knew very well, having been in her company a number of times. She asked, 'Mr. Hutchinson, can you lend me six pence?' I said I would not. She then walked on towards Thrawl-street, saying she must go and look for some money.

The man who was standing at the corner of Thrawl-street then came towards her and put his hand on her shoulder, and said something to her, the purport of which I did not hear, and they both burst out laughing. He put his hand again on her shoulder and they both walked slowly towards me. I walked on to the corner of Fashion-street, near the public-house. As they came by me his arm was still on her shoulder. He had a soft felt hat on and this was drawn down somewhat over his eyes. I put down my head to look him in the face and he turned and looked at me very sternly, and they walked across the road to Dorset-street. I followed them across and stood on the corner of Dorset-street. They stood at the corner of Miller's-court for about three minutes.

Kelly spoke to the man in a loud voice saying 'I have lost my handkerchief.' He pulled a red handkerchief out of his pocket and gave it to Kelly, and they both went up the court together. I went to look up the court to see if I could see them, but could not. I stood there for three-quarters of an hour to see if they came down again, but they did not, and so I went away.

My suspicions were aroused by seeing the man so well dressed, but I had no suspicion that he was the murderer. The man was about 5ft. 6in. in height and thirty-four or thirty-five years of age, with dark complexion and dark moustache turned up at the ends. He was wearing a long dark coat trimmed with astrakhan, a white collar with black necktie, in which was affixed a horseshoe pin. He wore a pair of dark spats with light buttons over buttoned boots, and displayed from his waistcoat a massive gold chain. His watch-chain had a big seal with a red stone hanging from it. He had a heavy moustache curled up and dark eyes and bushy eyebrows. He had no side whiskers and his chin was clean shaven. He looked like a foreigner.

I went up the court and stayed there a couple of minutes, but did not see any light in the house or hear any noise. I was out on Monday night until three o'clock looking for him. I could swear to the man anywhere. The man I saw carried a small parcel in his hand about eight inches long, and it had a strap round it. It looked as though it was covered with dark American cloth. He carried in his right hand, which he laid upon the woman's shoulder, a pair of brown kid gloves. He walked very softly. I believe that he lives in the neighbourhood, and I fancied that I saw him in Petticoat-lane on Sunday morning, but I was not certain.

I went down to the Shoreditch mortuary to-day (Tuesday) and recognised the body as being that of the woman Kelly whom I saw at two o'clock on Friday morning. Kelly did not seem to me to be drunk, but was a little spreeish: After I left the court I walked about all night, as the place where I usually sleep was closed. I am able to fix the time, as it was between ten and five minutes to two o'clock as I came by Whitechapel Church. When I left the corner of Miller's-court, the clock struck three. One policeman went by the Commercial-street end of Dorset-street while I was standing there, but not one came down Dorset-street. I saw one man go into a lodging-house in Dorset-street and no-one else. I have been looking for the man all day."

## FUNERAL OF MARY JANE KELLY

The remains of Mary Janet Kelly were carried on Monday morning from Shoreditch mortuary to the Roman Catholic Cemetery at Leytonstone for interment amidst a scene of turbulent excitement scarcely ever paralleled even in the annals of that densely-populated district where she met her death.

On the afternoon of the murder the body of the unfortunate woman was conveyed to the mortuary attached to St. Leonard's Church, Shoreditch, and there it remained until Monday. Since the inquest a great amount of sympathy for the fate of the deceased has been created, but it remained for Mr. H. Wilton, the sexton attached to Shoreditch Church, to put sympathy into a practical form, and as no relatives have appeared, he incurred the total cost of the funeral himself. Mr. Wilton has been sexton for over fifty years, and he provided the funeral as a mark of sympathy with the poor people of the neighbourhood.

The body was enclosed in a polished elm and oak coffin with metal mounts. On the coffin plate was engraved the words:- "Mary Jeanette Kelly, died 9th November, 1888, aged twenty-five years." Upon the coffin were two crowns of artificial flowers and a cross made up of heartsease. The coffin was carried in an open car drawn by two horses, and two coaches followed. An enormous crowd of people assembled at an early hour, completely blocking the thoroughfare, and a large number of police were engaged in keeping order.

The bell of St. Leonard's began tolling at noon, and the signal appeared to draw all the residents in the neighbourhood together. There was an enormous preponderance of women in the crowd. Scarcely any had any covering to their heads, and their tattered dresses indicated too surely that they belonged to the very class to which the murdered woman belonged. The wreaths upon the coffin bore cards inscribed with remembrances from friends using certain public-houses in common with the deceased.

As the coffin appeared, borne on the shoulders of four men, at the principal gate of the church, the crowd appeared to be moved greatly. Round the open car in which it was to be placed men and women struggled desperately to touch the coffin. Women with faces streaming with tears cried out "God forgive her!" and every man's head was bared in token of sympathy. The sight was quite remarkable and the emotion natural and unconstrained.

Two mourning coaches followed, one containing three and the other five persons. Joe Barnett was amongst them, with someone from McCarthy's, the landlord, and the others were women who had given evidence at the inquest. After a tremendous struggle the car, with the coffin fully exposed to view, set out at a very slow pace, all the crowd appearing to move off simultaneously in attendance. The traffic was blocked, of course, and the constables had great difficulty in obtaining free passage for the small procession through the mass of carts and vans and tramcars which blocked the road. The distance from Shoreditch Church to the cemetery at Leytonstone by road is about six miles, and the route traversed was Hackney-road, Cambridge-heath, Whitechapel-road, and Stratford.

In the Whitechapel-road the crowd on each side of the roadway was very great, and there was a considerable amount of emotion manifested. The appearance of the roadway throughout the whole journey was remarkable owing to the hundreds of men and women who escorted the coffin on either side, and who had to keep up a sharp trot in many places. But the crowd rapidly thinned away when, getting into the suburbs, the car and the coaches broke into a trot. Still the number of those who kept up was sufficient to spread the news in advance, and everywhere people stood in groups or crowded windows to see the *cortege* pass.

The cemetery was reached at two o'clock. The Rev. Father Columban, O.S.F., with two acolytes and a cross-bearer, met the body at the door of the little chapel of St. Patrick, and the coffin was carried at once to a grave in the north-eastern corner. Barnett and the poor women who had accompanied the funeral, knelt on the cold clay by the side of the grave while the service was read by Father Columban.

The coffin was incensed, lowered, and then sprinkled with holy water, and the simple ceremony ended. The floral ornaments were afterwards raised to be placed upon the grave, and the filling up was completed in a few moments and was watched by a small crowd of people.

(24.11.1888)

93

# THE MURDERS AT THE EAST END

*On a slow news week there was no shortage of Ripper stories to help boost circulation*

A Nottingham correspondent telegraphs that a remarkable letter, signed "Jack the Ripper's Pal," which has been handed over to the police, has been received by Mr. Robert Porter, of Hucknall Torkard, Notts.

The writer says he is a Nottingham man, and feels as if he could blow up all the dens in Whitechapel with the filthy women in them. There were, he adds, two concerned in the murders, and his "pal" taught him how to do it. He is now as bad as "Jack the Ripper," as he never feels frightened when cutting a woman up. When talking to a woman he can see the very devil; but he hoped the Lord will forgive him all his sins.

His pal is a Bavarian, whom he met on a steamship as he was returning from Colorado. Through being mesmerised he found out the other man's hideous calling. They have become very intimate, and his pal casts a sort of spell over him. His pal said he chucked two men overboard at sea. He is a wild wretch but a great magician and a clever man, with plenty of money. The writer, in conclusion, says he would be happier when he left England for good, but before then he and his pal would be heard of again…

On Wednesday a letter addressed to Chief Superintendent Hill, of the county constabulary, and bearing the Stoke-on-Trent and Burslem postmarks, was delivered at the police-station in the latter town. The letter purported to be a communication from the Whitechapel murderer, but the handwriting is said to differ in essential particulars from the facsimiles of other epistles published by the London police. Underneath the writing, which has the appearance of being in a disguised hand, there is a rough sketch of a dagger, and a second sketch the meaning of which is difficult to make out. The letter is couched in the following terms:

"Dear Boss, I now take to rite to you hoping to find you in good health as it leaves me very well at present and I have just come to Burslem and am going to kill eight more here and in Hanley. I have not got much time to right for Boss I rote this in the George public-house and I shall kill one to-day, and one the next day after. I have got a black suit of clothes and I saw all the police on Saturday and was talking to one of them but he did not know me at all. Dear Boss, I am very quick this time. My knife is eight inches long and will cut her arms off, next time I'll rite a letter with blood on my knife so no more from Jack the Ripper, please catch me if you can for you are very sharp. Signed, Jack the Ripper."

The letter is regarded as a silly hoax.

(8.12.1888)

# THE GIRL AND HER STEPFATHER'S MOUSTACHE

At the Southwark Police-court Patrick Lonegan, living at 184, Southwark-bridge-road, appeared to a summons charging him with assaulting his wife Ellen on

THE GIRL AND HER STEPFATHER'S MOUSTACHE.

the fifth of October. The complainant was an elderly woman, who stated her age to be fifty-five, and the defendant, who has been married about three years, is a young man, who did not look more than twenty-seven.

The wife stated that on the 7th ult. she had a few words with her husband with regard to his conduct with her daughter, who was nineteen years old, when he struck her a violent blow in the mouth, causing her to fall, and whilst on the ground he pushed a heavy chair over, which fell upon and bruised her about the ribs. About three months ago she charged her husband with assaulting her, and he was sentenced to a month's hard labour. When he came out of prison she allowed him to come home again and since then he had repeatedly assaulted her.

Defendant: What were the words about?

Complainant: I came into the room and found my daughter looking over you when you were in the chair, and she was curling your moustache. I saw her do it a lot of times.

Miss Booth (a daughter of the complainant by a former marriage): Oh, what a lie!

Miss Marian Booth, a rather prepossessing young woman, stylishly dressed and wearing her hair down her back, was called by the defendant, and said ever since her stepfather had been out of prison her mother was always nagging at him, and calling him a coward. Her mother was always getting drunk, and they led a most miserable life at home, and her father had frequently to pawn his clothes to buy food. She was quite sure her mother was not assaulted. She denied the curling of the moustache altogether.

Mr. Fanwick (to the defendant): I shall bind you over in the sum of £20, and you will have to find two sureties in £10 each to keep the peace for six months, or in default twenty-one days. The defendant was removed in the van to Wandsworth.

(02.11.1889)

## A SAUSAGE MAKER'S PONIES

In the Lord Mayor's Court, on Wednesday, the case of Harris v. Carter Paterson and Co. (Limited) was tried before the Assistant-Judge (Mr. Roxburgh) and a jury. The plaintiff, Mr. W. Harris, of 3, St. John-street, West Smithfield, sued the defendants, the well-known carriers, to recover compensation for injuries inflicted upon a valuable pony by the alleged negligence of the defendant's servants.

Mr. Wildey Wright, in opening the case, explained that Mr. Harris had a large number of small carts for conveying sausages wherever wanted. These carts had pictures with a large gold pig ridden by a man who was winning the pork sausage Derby. These carts were drawn by handsome thoroughbred ponies, and it was one of these ponies which was injured on the occasion in question.

THE SAUSAGEMAKER'S PONY.

Mr. W. Harris, the plaintiff, was called, and stated that he bred all his own ponies. They were all freemen of the City, because they were born in the City.

Mr. Wildey Wright: This was a very pretty piebald pony?

The Plaintiff: It was a parti-coloured entire pony. The ponies are particularly valuable to my business, because people know them whenever they see them. This one took a prize at Olympia two years ago.

Continuing his evidence the plaintiff said that he had three other ponies, for each of which he would refuse one hundred guineas. After the accident the injured one was sold for £1.15s.

Mr. Ogle (for the defence): I suppose he is identified with sausages more than ever now?

The defence was that the pony was worth only fifteen guineas. Carl North said he was horse manager to the defendants, who had 2,200 horses. He valued the pony at £5 before the accident.

Mr. Wright: You don't deny that it was a prettily-marked pony?

Witness: It was marked like a calf.

Other expert evidence having been given, the jury found a verdict for the plaintiff for £35.15s., including fifteen guineas paid into court.

(09.11.1889)

## DESPERATE AFFRAY WITH DETECTIVES

George William Parke, thirty-five, a laundryman residing at Loftus-road, Shepherd's-bush, was charged with assaulting Henry Marshall, a Scotland-yard detective-inspector, in the execution of his duty and preventing the lawful apprehension of a man named A.H.Graham…

Inspector Marshall said he went with Detective-sergeant Wheateley, X division, about eight o'clock on Saturday night, to the house of the prisoner, to arrest a man named Graham, on a warrant for being concerned with some of the prisoners in custody for conspiracy. It was only fair to the prisoner Parke that he (witness) should explain that he was dressed as a baker's man, with white cap, floury coat, and apron, and on his back carried a baker's basket with loaves and bread in it (laughter).

On knocking at the door he was admitted by a boy, and witness pretended that he had some bread to deliver, and some conversation ensued about the ordering of the bread. While that was going on Graham (the man wanted) came running down the stairs accompanied by a younger man, and as soon as Graham had come near enough to him, witness seized him and said, "I am Inspector Marshall of Scotland Yard." Both he

and Parke knew him well enough. Parke at once struck witness on the arm with his fist, and then all three men set on him and tried to make him loosen his hold on Graham. Some of them turned out all the lights and they were in total darkness. Somehow witness was literally carried along some distance by the men until they came to a door, where he got fixed. All through the struggle he sustained his grip of Graham and pulled him along with him.

At last the man broke away from him, and somebody in the house let loose two dogs, a large collie and a fox-terrier, and they came barking down the stairs in a great fury and flew at witness. But singularly enough, while the dogs worried witness only, one of them bit the prisoner Parke on the thigh, and tore his trousers. During the struggle, aided by the darkness, Graham got out of the way.

Witness went out and got the assistance of Sergeant Wheatley and they got into the house again. They groped about in the darkness and presently they came upon someone they thought to be Graham and seized him, but when they were about to get a light they discovered that it was the prisoner Parke. Witness shouted to Sergeant Wheatley to run upstairs and search the place, but the dogs were set on to him, and they were so furious and menacing that Wheatley was held at bay for a considerable time. That delay allowed Graham and the other man to make good their escape. Sergeant Wheatley arrested a woman and witness told the prisoner Parke that he would be arrested for assaulting him and for obstructing him in the apprehension of a man...

The prisoner was remanded

(18.01.1890)

## MECHANICAL FORTUNE TELLING

At the North London Police-court, on Tuesday, Edward Bianchi, forty-five, confectioner, of High-street, Stoke Newington, was charged before Mr. Haden Corser with using a mechanical apparatus as a device for telling fortunes.

The machine was brought into court. A female figure, with an outstretched finger, was made to revolve, and ultimately stop before one of the many "foolish sentences" – as the magistrate described them – written round the disc. The prisoner said it was not his machine – a company placed that and others about and he took a commission on the takings.

The magistrate: Foolish people spend their money and the company takes the profit.

Constable Prince deposed to watching the machine and seeing children and servant maids putting pennies in. He himself put two pennies in, and the finger pointed to "Prosperity awaits you."

Mr Corser: There is not much of a fortune in standing drinks (Laughter). But you have here which is very good advice and would be a well laid out penny if followed, "Drop drinking spirits." I shall bind this man to come up for judgement if called upon. I shall not convict an isolated case. But if the treasury takes up the prosecution of the whole thing then the accused can be dealt with.

(19.07.1890)

# EXECUTION OF MRS. PEARCEY

*Twenty-four-year-old Mary Pearcey was hanged for the murder of her lover's wife and eighteen-month-old daughter. Mrs. Hogg's body was found with her throat cut from ear to ear on Crossfield Road, Hampstead. The daughter was discovered suffocated in a rubbish dump about a mile away. It was generally believed that Mrs.Pearcey lured her love rival to her home and hacked the young mother to death. The next day she bundled the body into a pram, and, as a result, suffocated the daughter.*

*When police searched Mrs. Pearcey's home she began playing the piano and singing loudly enough to wake the dead. As more and more bloody evidence came to light the demented pianist played ever more furiously. When asked to explain the bloodstains on a chopper, Mary Pearcey sang back her reply that she had been "Killing mice, killing mice, killing mice!"*

The strenuous efforts made on behalf of Mrs. Pearcey proved unsuccessful. They were continued until the last practical moment, and strong hopes were entertained

that the results of the medical inquiry, which was held on Friday afternoon, would have been of such a character that the Home Secretary would have felt justified in not ordering the enforcement of the extreme penalty. But this was not the case, and the poor woman was left for execution.

Mrs. Pearcey was visited on Saturday by a relative and friend of her mother, who is an aged woman, and unable personally to visit the prisoner. The friend was permitted an interview with Mrs. Pearcey, and states that there was a considerable change in her appearance, and that when she came to the wire grating to speak she was bent nearly double. Her face was wan and pale, and she trembled so that she seemed scarcely able to speak.

She stated that there had been inquiries as to how certain matters had got into the newspapers, and that the authorities had given orders that nothing further was to be allowed to transpire. She expressed herself as resigned to her fate, whatever it may be, but she had forebodings that the worst was near, because she had received an intimation from the authorities of the prison that if she desired any of her friends to see her they were to be at the gaol by ten o'clock on Monday morning, and, if there was no respite, that she must then be prepared to take a final farewell of all of them. She added an instruction that her mother was to be at Newgate by ten o'clock at the latest, as she was told that the business of the preparations would then begin. She thought, however, there was one thing which the authorities ought to grant to her, as it was her last request, and that was that she might be allowed to see and embrace her mother in a room by themselves, without the iron bars being between them, and when no one was by. She added, "Give my love to my dear mother, and tell her how I love her, but that I speak the truth when I tell her I am innocent." The relative then said, "If you are innocent, why don't you say who did the murder?" To this Mrs. Pearcey replied, "No."

The mother, being told of this, said her daughter would not do so if she had ever promised not to do so. The friend then asked her if Hogg did it, and she said, "No; Hogg was not in it."

The Central News says: Despite a bitter frost, a sulphury fog, and slippery streets small knots of people commenced gathering in the Old Bailey before seven o'clock on Tuesday morning to satisfy a morbid curiosity in seeing the black flag hoisted over the walls of Newgate as a symbol to the world that Mrs. Pearcey had paid the penalty of the law for the atrocious murder of Mrs. Hogg and her infant child at Hampstead. The solemn tolling of the dying woman's funeral bell had no effect upon the crowd, not the slightest sympathy being felt by the members of her own sex.

At one minute before eight o'clock a yell from the crowd proclaimed the fact that the black flag was hoisted, and, directly after the crowd gave vent to their feelings in a loud cheer, which was taken up and repeated as the scattered groups gathered into one compact mass in the Old Bailey. Excited talk was general, and fierce delight was expressed when it was found that the unhappy creature had paid the penalty of her crimes.

(27.12.1890)

## LATEST WHITECHAPEL MURDER

The poor creature was younger than the other victims, and in several reports more easily to be recognised. This is the official description of the body:- "A woman age about twenty-five, length 5ft., hair and eyes brown, complexion pale, dressed in black skirt and satin bodice, brown petticoat, grey stays, black diagonal jacket, trimmed with blue, white chemise and drawers, striped stockings, button boots. She wore a black ribbon round her neck. In her left ear was a black vulcanite earring, the fellow to which was in her pocket. She wore a black crape hat, and carried another similar hat in the folds of her dress. In the pocket of her dress were found three pieces of black crape, an old striped stocking, and a comb. The lobe of the left ear has been torn as if by an earring – an old wound. All the clothing is old and dirty."

Importance is attached by the Press Association, as suggesting a new clue, to the finding of a woman's hat on the body besides the crape headgear which the victim had evidently been wearing. This fact has caused surprise to the police, for it goes to support the suggestion that the crime might have been perpetrated by a woman, or, at any rate, by a man in female attire…

(21.02.1891)

## NEARLY LYNCHED BY WOMEN

Dr. W. Wynn Wentcott held an inquest at Paddington Coroner's court, on the body of Laura Hollands, aged thirty-three, who was found drowned in the Regent's Canal, Maida-vale on Tuesday morning.

The evidence showed that death was due to suffocation by drowning. The deceased's hat was found hanging to a post beside the canal. The body was got out with drags, and Dr. George Bird, who examined it, said the deceased had a wound on the inside of her lower lip. Only fourpence in money was found in her possession.

Mrs. Rose Sutton, of 14, Crompton-park, Paddington, said she had been in service with the deceased, who was then a respectable, well-conducted girl. The deceased married Henry Hellafuls, a Civil Service clerk; but four years ago they separated, mainly, witness believed, in consequence of her husband's want of fidelity, and because of his misconduct.

Afterwards Mrs. Hollands went to live with a house painter named George Burgess, who had treated her most brutally, and lived upon the proceeds of her prostitution ever since. (Sensation.) Witness last saw her old fellow-servant alive on the preceding Thursday, when she complained of Burgess's violence, of being taken to Maidenhead by him, and thrown destitute upon the

# A MAN NEARLY LYNCHED BY WOMEN AT PADDINGTON.

streets there to get money for both. She said, "George is a beast to me, and life is not worth living."

Rose Haydon, single woman, 19, North-street, Edgware-road, deposed that the deceased had no settled home, and witness was with her walking Edgware-road until two o'clock in the morning, trying to persuade her not to drown herself, as she threatened to do because of Burgess's ill-usage. The injury to her lower lip was, witness knew, the result of this man's violence. The deceased on Tuesday morning said, "George shall never have the pleasure of hitting me again," threw her umbrella to witness saying, "that's for you Rose," and then ran away. Witness never afterwards saw her alive.

The Coroner: Do you believe she drowned herself through this man's violence?

Witness: I am sure of it. She used to keep him when he was out of work, which was almost always, and when he worked and earned money he would knock her about if she asked for any. A more respectable girl of her class never passed down Edgware-road. She has a mother living near Dublin.

George Burgess, who seemed under the influence of drink, and spoke laughingly, elected to give evidence after being cautioned by the coroner. He said he left the deceased in Marylebone-road, shortly before midnight on Monday, and went home to his lodging direct; that he did not leave the house until ten the next morning; and that the landlady's son, who slept in the same room with him, could prove this. He should, he said, have married the deceased if she had not already been married.

The Coroner: How came you to knock her about?

Witness: I did not knock her about unless under provocation.

What do you mean by provocation?

The provocation was through drink.

But you drink yourself.

I know I do.

You would not have liked her to knock you about because you drank?

But she did.

Who injured her lip?

She did herself. I did not drown her.

Rose Haydon: No, you did not drown her, but you murdered her, nevertheless.

Burgess began laughing and was rebuked by a juror who said, "This is not a laughing but a very serious matter."

I didn't take her to the canal and put her in.

Haydon: If you had not marked her in the mouth she would never have done it. You nearly murdered her when she could not get you money.

The jury found that the deceased "committed suicide when in distress of mind owing to the cruelty and ill-treatment of George Burgess, the man with whom she lived, whose conduct the jury condemn in the strongest manner, and only regret that they are unable to send him to another court for punishment."

The coroner remarked that words of loathing and detestation would be wasted upon a person like Burgess, who was about to speak, when the coroner said: the jury don't wish to hear you. You may go and consider yourself lucky that you are not sent for trial.

Burgess then left, but outside the court he was beset by a number of furious women, by whom he was roughly handled, and from whom he had much difficulty in escaping.

(10.10.1891)

# CRIMINAL AND SOCIAL HISTORY THEY DIDN'T DARE TEACH YOU AT SCHOOL!

TITLE: **THROUGH THE KEYHOLE**
AUTHOR: **STEVE JONES**
ISBN: **1-870000-02-1**
SIZE: **A4**
PAGES: **104**
ILLUSTRATIONS/PHOTOS: **109**
PRICE: **£6.99**
NOTES: **AVAILABLE IN JAPANESE.**

A peek at private lives, from prince to pauper, in the eighteenth and nineteenth centuries. 'Through the Keyhole' reveals the secrets of what went on behind locked doors in workhouses, slums and palaces – with detailed court accounts of adultery and sexual scandal. In later chapters we look at how the masses spent their limited leisure time in pubs and penny playhouses.

TITLE: **LONDON... THE SINISTER SIDE**
AUTHOR: **STEVE JONES**
ISBN: **1-87000-000-5**
SIZE: **A4**
PAGES: **88**
ILLUSTRATIONS/PHOTOS: **104**
PRICE: **£6.99**
NOTES: **AVAILABLE IN JAPANESE.**

Our first and best-selling book which has been in print since 1986 with reprints well into double figures. Topics covered range from early executions to the Kray Twins. 15 pages are devoted to the hunt for Jack the Ripper and the book illustrated with over 100 photographs and pictures.

TITLE: **CAPITAL PUNISHMENTS**
AUTHOR: **STEVE JONES**
ISBN: **1-870000-03-X**
SIZE: **A4**
PAGES: **104**
ILLUSTRATIONS/PHOTOS: **106**
PRICE: **£7.99**
NOTES: **AVAILABLE IN JAPANESE.**

A detailed look at a variety of cases coming before the 'beak' in Victorian times. Assault and wife-beating were only too common following serious sessions in the ale-houses. The book follows those convicted into the horrors of the Victorian prison system where silence was often the rule and the food 'scarce fit for hogs'. Many of the stories of the atrocious conditions are related by the prisoners themselves.

TITLE: **WICKED LONDON**
AUTHOR: **STEVE JONES**
ISBN: **1-870000-01-3**
SIZE: **A4**
PAGES: **96**
ILLUSTRATIONS/PHOTOS: **96**
PRICE: **£6.99**
NOTES: **AVAILABLE IN JAPANESE.**

In two parts. The first half of the book examines the most notorious murder cases in the capital including Dr. Crippen, Christie, Haig – 'the acid-bath' murderer and many more. The second half is centred around social life – food, drink and leisure – and conflict within the capital, including chapters on the often violent struggle of the women's movement and tragic tales of the Blitz.

TITLE: **IN DARKEST LONDON**
AUTHOR: **STEVE JONES**
ISBN: **1-870000-04-8**
SIZE: **A4**
PAGES: **88**
ILLUSTRATIONS/PHOTOS: **79**
PRICE: **£6.99**

The book covers the period 1900-39 and relates first hand stories of prostitutes, criminals and backstreet abortionists. Details of the bombing raids in world war one are followed by tales of the General Strike of 1926 and an in depth look at Mosley's racist marches in the East End that resulted in serious violence and disruption. Light relief is provided with the extraordinary life of the prostitute's padre who ended his days in a lion's cage.

TITLE: **WHEN THE LIGHTS WENT DOWN**
AUTHOR: **STEVE JONES**
ISBN: **1-870000-05-6**
SIZE: **A4**
PAGES: **104**
ILLUSTRATIONS/PHOTOS: **91**
PRICE: **£7.99**

We've all heard the stories about the civilian population during WW2 pulling together, singing patriotic songs in crowded air-raid shelters and accepting the wartime privations in good heart. Indeed many did, but there was a sizeable minority who were determined to help themselves rather than their country. German bombers facilitated entry to other people's houses, and undercover of the blackout, looters set out on their gruesome treasure trove. Both crime figures and the prison population rose as offenders from black-marketeers to murderers sought to profit from the chaotic conditions.

TITLE: **NOTTINGHAM... THE SINISTER SIDE**
AUTHOR: **STEVE JONES**
ISBN: **1-870000-06-4**
SIZE: **A4**
PAGES: **104**
ILLUSTRATIONS/PHOTOS: **110**
PRICE: **£7.99**

Although internationally famous for being the home of Britain's most famous outlaw, Robin Hood, Nottingham, like all large cities, has housed tens of thousands of lawbreakers with no intention whatsoever of giving to the poor. The most infamous murders include 'Nurse Waddingham who poisoned two of her patients for their inheritance, and Herbert Mills, who executed 'the perfect murder' in order to sell his story to the newspapers – both were hanged.

TITLE: **LANCASHIRE LASSES... THEIR LIVES AND CRIMES**
AUTHOR: **STEVE JONES**
ISBN: **1-870000-07-2**
SIZE: **A4**
PAGES: **104**
ILLUSTRATIONS/PHOTOS: **107**
PRICE: **£7.99**

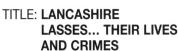

Life for Lancashire lasses in Victorian times often followed the path from mill or mine to marriage and maternity. On average they fell pregnant eight times and would raise their children as they themselves had been raised – in grinding poverty.

The temptation to escape the hardships was too great for many. Some would turn to crime, some to the bottle and some to both. Offenders were paraded in the dock on charges ranging from picking pockets to prostitution.

TITLE: **BIRMINGHAM... THE SINISTER SIDE**
AUTHOR: **STEVE JONES**
ISBN: **1-870000-14-5**
SIZE: **A4**
PAGES: **104**
ILLUSTRATIONS/PHOTOS: **133**
PRICE: **£7.99**

NOTES: **THIS BOOK IS EXTREMELY POPULAR, THE FIRST PRINT SELLING OUT IN ELEVEN WEEKS. HAS BEEN FEATURED ON SEVERAL RADIO AND TELEVISION PROGRAMMES.**

'Pickpockets, petty thieves, prostitutes, drunks, murderers and wife-beaters galore people its pages staring back at the reader from police 'mug-shots' with grim resignation, pathos or rebellion in their eyes sandwiched between spine-chilling 'penny-dreadful' illustrations portraying scenes of red murder of callous brutality, each of which for a fleeting moment in time, shocked the un-shockable!' (Black Country Bugle).

TITLE: **NORTHUMBERLAND AND DURHAM... THE SINISTER SIDE**
AUTHOR: **STEVE JONES**
ISBN: **1-870000-49-8**
SIZE: **A4**
PAGES: **104**
ILLUSTRATIONS/PHOTOS: **100**
PRICE: **£7.99**

With tales from Berwick to Darlington, petty-theft to mass-murder join us in an uncensored trip back to Victorian times in Northumberland and old County Durham. Stories of Britain's wickedest woman plus many tales from the courtrooms, slums and ale-houses so popular in the North-East.

TITLE: **MANCHESTER... THE SINISTER SIDE**
AUTHOR: **STEVE JONES**
ISBN: **1-870000-09-9**
SIZE: **A4**
PAGES: **104**
ILLUSTRATIONS/PHOTOS: **103**
PRICE: **£7.99**

With the presence of over 100 photographs and illustrations, join us in a trip back in time to meet the incorrigible rogues, vagabonds and thieves in Victorian Manchester and the atrocious conditions endured by the vast majority of the population.

# WICKED PUBLICATIONS

Lavishly illustrated and studiously researched, our original stories and photographs would certainly interest students (GCSE to degree level), local historians, social historians, genealogists and criminologists – but above all they are aimed at the general reader.

To date our satisfied customers total over 250,000.

## TERMS AND CONDITIONS

### INDIVIDUAL SALES

We supply orders to the general public at the prices listed below. Wicked Publications pay all postage and packing within the U.K. and books will be sent within twenty-four hours of an order being received. Cheques should be made payable to **Wicked Publications**. At the moment we cannot accept credit cards. If you would like the books signed or dedicated please mention this with the order.

### BUSINESS

We have accounts with all major booksellers and museum/visitor shops. Our general terms are 35% sale or return, if they don't sell we will take the book back if in resalable condition. We can confidently make this promise as returns over ten years have been minimal. We may give better terms for large orders or swift payment or to regular customers, everything is negotiable, please phone.

# ORDER FORM

PLEASE SEND ORDER ALONG WITH CHEQUE TO **WICKED PUBLICATIONS AT 222, HIGHBURY ROAD, BULWELL, NOTTINGHAM NG6 9FE, ENGLAND. TEL: 0115 975 6828.**

| TITLE | PRICE | NO OF COPIES |
|---|---|---|
| LONDON... THE SINISTER SIDE | £6.99 | |
| WICKED LONDON | £6.99 | |
| THROUGH THE KEYHOLE | £6.99 | |
| CAPITAL PUNISHMENTS | £7.99 | |
| IN DARKEST LONDON | £6.99 | |
| WHEN THE LIGHTS WENT DOWN | £7.99 | |
| NOTTINGHAM... THE SINISTER SIDE | £7.99 | |
| LANCASHIRE LASSES... THEIR LIVES AND CRIMES | £7.99 | |
| MANCHESTER... THE SINISTER SIDE | £7.99 | |
| BIRMINGHAM... THE SINISTER SIDE | £7.99 | |
| NORTHUMBERLAND AND DURHAM... THE SINISTER SIDE | £7.99 | |
| **\*Postage** (where applicable) | £ | \*(ALL POSTAGE IS FREE WITHIN THE U.K. ADD £1.50 PER BOOK MAINLAND EUROPE AND £3 U.S.A., CANADA, AUSTRALIA AND NEW ZEALAND). |
| **TOTAL** | £ | |

Name.................................................................................................................

Address............................................................................................................

...........................................................................................................................

...........................................................................................................................

..................................................Post Code ...................................